Discover The Angels

Alison Wynne-Ryder

Author of the bestselling *The Quirky Medium*

Alison Wynne-Ryder © 2025

All rights reserved in accordance with the Copyright, Designs and Patents Act 1988.

No parts of this publication may be reproduced, stored in a retrieval system, or transmitted in any form or by any means whatsoever without the prior permission of the publisher.
A record of this publication is available from the British Library.

ISBN 978-1-910027-66-0

Typesetting and cover design by Titanium Design Ltd

www.titaniumdesign.co.uk

Cover images licensed by Adobe Stock

Published by Local Legend
https://local-legend.co.uk

Dedication

To my beloved soulmate, John, now in spirit and flying with the angels.

"It all comes right in the end." (John Ellis Wynne, 1955 – 2023)

Acknowledgements

I am grateful to Nigel Peace of Local Legend for always believing in me.
Also a big shout out to everyone who contributed to this book
by sharing their true stories and love of all things angelic.
Last, but never least, thank you to the angels for everything.
What would I do without you?

https://local-legend.co.uk

About the author

Alison Wynne-Ryder is known as 'the Angel Lady with a Difference', her quirky sense of humour evident in everything she does. She helps others to embrace the love of the angels in their homes and personal spaces, to bring peace and positivity into their lives through her workshops, healing sessions and online teaching.

She is a clairvoyant medium of international fame, the star of the TV show *Rescue Mediums,* and an Usui Reiki Master Teacher, practising and teaching Reiki for more than two decades.

Alison's first book, *The Quirky Medium*, is a worldwide bestseller and she has written many articles for spiritual magazines as well as regular spiritual columns in the local Press.

She now lives in southern Spain with her beloved rescue dog, Ella.

Alison's website is https://www.thequirkymedium.com/

Previous Publications
The Quirky Medium (Local Legend, 2012)
ISBN 978-1-907203-47-3

Contents

Foreword		1
1	Angels and Deities	3
2	Angels Today	15
3	Bringing in the Light	29
4	Communicating With the Angels	39
5	Beliefs About Angels	51
6	The Angelic Hierarchy	63
7	Questions and Answers	75
8	The Healing Ambience	89
9	Elements and Earth Angels	101
10	Angel Magic	111
11	Meditation and Prayer	125
12	Afterlife	141
Addendum		155

Foreword

*"An angel's wing beats at every window,
but only the listening hear and rise."*
(Muriel Strode)

This book has been written for you, whether you are a complete beginner or someone who wishes to connect with angels at a deeper level. I hope it touches your heart.

The angels have always been part of my life. Whenever I've been scared – particularly by ghosts! – I've called for help and the angels have never let me down. They have helped me in my personal life as well as during my work as a clairvoyant medium, particularly during spirit rescues. In times of turmoil and darkness, I've always known there was someone out there looking after me. I can honestly say that without angels' divine support and protection, I would be in a very different place in mind, body and soul.

But this book isn't all about me! It includes the most awe-inspiring true life stories from many others, all of whom have given me permission to share their phenomenal divine encounters with you. I hope that these accounts will help you to take a step closer to believing in angels and welcoming them into your life.

1
Angels and deities

*"Persons who are visited by the angel
quiver with a thrill unknown to the rest of mankind."*
(Gaston Leroux)

So much has been written and passed down throughout history, and in every culture, about mankind praying to otherworldly beings and angels, in different shapes and forms.

Going back to the last days of the Stone Age, Neolithic Man had ultimate faith in Mother Nature. They worshipped the fertility of the land, believing in all that she was and still is, the ultimate provider and epitome of life itself. To thank her for all that she brought to their lives, in the only way they knew how, they prayed to the sun, the moon and the stars as well as to the natural elements of water, earth, fire and air.

People who lived off the land also gave thanks to the animals they hunted, as without them they would have no food, water or shelter. Many archaeological digs have unearthed the most amazing ancient artefacts, items that helped early men to develop their lives. Examples are handmade tools made out of stone or wood, such as spears, bows, arrows and axes used for harvesting crops, killing animals for food and cutting down trees.

Some of the most intriguing items, however, are predominantly handmade feminine figures that may have represented the Great Mother goddess. There are fish, snakes or birds representing water and air deities, earth goddesses, figures of pregnant women to represent the fertility goddess and the waxing and waning of the moon. Collectively, these feminine figures have been described as 'Venuses' after the Roman goddess of love and fertility.

Perhaps the worship of nature was the origin of other forms of deities found in mythology, such as the supernatural beings known as fairies or 'angels of the forest', and the legends of mermaids, or 'angels of the sea'. Later, monuments were also built in ways that linked with the cycle of life, from the waxing and waning of the moon, the movement of the sun and the changing of the seasons, bringing a magical sense to everything that mankind believed in.

One of the earliest well-known winged deities, around 1300 BCE, was the Sumerian protective goddess Lamma, later known in the Assyrian civilisation as the Lamassu. It was an imposing figure with a human head representing intelligence, the body of a bull to denote strength and large outstretched eagle's wings for freedom. Many also believed that the winged bull was made up of the astronomical constellations of the zodiac, which was how early civilisations determined the time of year.

The Lamassu was known to ward off evil so its statues were carved from stone and often placed at the entrances of palaces. This was done not just to protect the king but also to remind the people of his power; anyone entering the palace would have to walk between two of the statues. They were so formidable that some believed them to be alive.

Centuries later, the Roman Lares were deities worshipped by homeowners who believed they would protect their crops, homes and bring blessings on their lives. It is thought that each household had one particular Lare, usually a departed ancestor who had led a good life. In death they were believed to become divine beings, buried in the home and worshipped each morning. Whenever there were celebrations in the family, offerings were made to the Lares such as grain, wheat, grapes and wine.

The Romans certainly believed in spiritual worlds. During the festival of Lemuria in May, people would cleanse themselves with fresh water as they spat black beans out and recited a mantra such as, "As I cast these beans, I am and mine are redeemed." This was done to stop their deceased loved ones from haunting them and to keep evil spirits from their home, since they would follow the beans and leave the living in peace!

The Valkyries are famous in Norse mythology and the name means 'chooser of the slain'. They were believed to be beautiful deities who served the god Odin, riding on horseback amongst soldiers during battle and deciding their fate, then guiding the deceased souls along one of two paths. Half of them went to Odin's Valhalla, to the Hall of Heroes where they came back to life in the evening and celebrated by drinking all night.

The other half were guided along a different path, to a place called Folkvangr which was ruled by the goddess Freyja. Here would be a home, Sessrumnir or 'room of many seats', for the elderly soldiers and those who were very sick, so they could rest before going over to the spirit world. Some believed that Freyja was a Valkyrie herself.

With the rising influence of monotheistic religions, the powerful beings of the spiritual worlds became thought of as angels. One of the earliest references to angels, more or less as we would recognise them, is in the ancient faith of Zoroastrianism. This was named after a reforming Persian prophet, Zoroaster, also known as Zarathushtra, who lived some time between the years 1500 and 1000 BCE. His teachings were recorded in a book called *The Gathas*. It is said that an angel came before him and introduced him to Ahura Mazda, an ancient god or supreme creator, who spoke to him in visions and dreams about the hierarchy of angels, the god's messengers.

As belief in Christianity spread across the world, the images and statues of angels in galleries and churches with beautiful stained glass windows gave comfort to those who worshipped there. We have always needed to feel protected and cared for.

Only two archangels, Michael and Gabriel, are named in the Bible but there are references to angelic beings throughout. The earliest account may be in the Book of Job (38: v.4-7) where God tells Job he should have had more confidence in divine greatness.

"Where were you when I laid the foundation of the Earth, when the morning stars sung together and all the sons of God shouted for joy?"

Many believe that the morning stars that sung together is a reference to the host of angels that sang in happy unison as God created the Earth.

The ranks of angels were not described within the Bible in ways we are familiar with nowadays, as portrayed in paintings, books or films. This could be because the image of an angel would have been described by word of mouth and therefore distorted over time. Equally, perhaps many people still clung to the old mythical beliefs about supernatural beings.

For example, in the Bible the Cherubim have four faces and four wings whereas the Seraphim are said to have six wings, four to cover their heads and feet, and two for flying. There are a few other lesser known and rather strange angels mentioned such as the Malakim, described as being messengers of God and who looked like human beings without wings yet were very fierce. The most bizarre by far are the Ophanim, said to look like interlocking golden wheels covered in hundreds of eyes. They guarded the throne of the Divine and, even though they didn't have wings, they moved themselves about until they could fly up into the air.

Of course, one of the most famous stories ever told is that of Archangel Gabriel appearing before Mary to inform her that she would bear a son who would do great things. A very surprised Mary's reply was, "How can this be, since I am a virgin?" Gabriel told her that she would be guided by the Holy Spirit, and her child would be known as the Son of God. Christians still celebrate the birth of Jesus on the 25th December, now known as Christmas. Although it may have lost its original meaning for some, church services across the world still portray the nativity and give thanks through hymns and prayer for the birth of Jesus.

Later, an angel would appear before Jesus himself as he prayed in the Garden of Gethsemane before his arrest, "Father, if You are willing, take this cup from me. Yet not my will but Yours be done." At this point, an angel sent from God came to strengthen and comfort him.

The Book of Revelation completes the New Testament in the Bible. Written by John the Divine, it announces everything that God relayed to Jesus so he in turn could share God's words with believers. In layman's terms the Book tells of the fight between good and evil. Much of it is in mystical language, culminating in dire warnings of Armageddon and the Last Judgement.

Revelation is full of references to angels as agents of God's will. They are said to be able to control the elements: in Chapter 7, four angels are described as holding back the four winds of the Earth whilst in other passages angels are described as having power over fire and the waters. In Chapter 15, seven angels are said to emerge from the temple with vials full of God's wrath, later to be poured out, bringing God's judgement upon the wicked. Another seven angels will later sound trumpets in a series of events leading to the Apocalypse.

There are certainly, it seems, a lot of angels! John describes a vision of them, worshipping at God's throne. "Then I looked, and I heard around the throne and the living creatures and the elders the voice of many angels, numbering myriads of myriads and thousands of thousands."

Jeanne d'Arc, better known to us as Joan of Arc, was a young peasant woman born around 1412 CE at Domrémy in northeast France during the latter part of The Hundred Years War with England. Joan started to hear disembodied voices when she was twelve years-old, especially, she believed, that of Archangel Michael. He told her not to be afraid because God had sent him to protect her as she had a powerful mission to complete. This would be revealed with divine timing.

Later, Joan would see Archangel Michael in all his glory,

surrounded by other heavenly angels, and learn that she was to defend France in battle and must rely on the guidance of God. She told this to Robert de Baudricourt, a local lord, who dismissed her accounts and sent her back to her father. However, she was persistent and soon other people believed her.

At about sixteen years-old, Joan went to see Prince Charles of Valois and described Archangel Michael's prophecies. At first he laughed when she told him she was to lead France into victory over England. But when she told him some personal information that no-one else knew, he believed her.

Charles sent her to the Siege of Orléans as part of a relief army, where she donned armour and wielded a banner, inspiring the demoralised French army. The English soon abandoned the siege and were pursued north and defeated. The French army advanced to Reims, where Charles was crowned King Charles VII, with Joan at his side.

However, as had also been prophesised by Archangel Michael, she was captured by the English and tried on accusations of heresy, including blaspheming by wearing men's clothes, having demonic visions and refusing to submit to the Church. She was declared guilty and burned at the stake on 30th May, 1431, aged about nineteen. Throughout this time, though, she still saw the visions of Archangel Michael, who gave her comfort. Twenty-five years later, the verdict was overturned and Joan became revered as a martyr. She was canonised as a saint in 1920 by Pope Benedict XV and is now known as the patron saint of soldiers and of France.

Nearly all encounters between people and angels are very personal. But there is one famous story in which hundreds of men all saw the same great host of angels. On August 23rd, 1914, the British Expeditionary Forces found themselves in the muddy fields of Mons as German troops swept through Belgium. The British retreated towards the river Marne but were in a desperate plight, fearing for their lives. Many of them turned to prayer.

What happened next has become the legend of the White

Cavalry. Suddenly the heavens opened and an army of angelic soldiers dressed in white descended between the two armies and forced the Germans back, their horses terrified.

There have been several different descriptions of the event. One British soldier said, "We saw a glimmering golden glow, a pure white horse, it was Saint George… He had armour on and a massive shield and lance in his hand. He spoke and said, 'Messieurs de Saint George'." Others described the event as a cloud of light, as winged horsemen led by Archangel Michael or even as the English knights of Agincourt firing arrows at the enemy.

Did these soldiers, in their extreme state of fear, really see an angelic host? We can never know the full truth, but something very paranormal happened that day. A year later, a British officer published an account in the journal *Light*, confirming that 'a huge, strange cloud descended from the sky between both armies and protected the British…'

Throughout the ages there have been many different images of angels in art. In the Middle Ages and up to Victorian times, painters usually portrayed angels as beautiful humanistic beings with blond, curly hair and large, outstretched feathered wings, showing them as messengers that fly between Heaven and Earth. Perhaps the wings also symbolised protection, love and courage. Angelic beings were also shown with a golden halo, representing their special energy field or aura.

Naturally, most paintings of angels had religious themes although in the Renaissance period, the 'age of rebirth', some artists expressed more freedom and might include hidden meanings in their work, perhaps their own interests or something that was unique about themselves.

A good example is *The Music Angel* by the Italian artist Rosso

Fiorentino. At first, the painting seems to be exactly as the title describes, an angel playing a lute. However, Fiorentino gave his little angel red hair, just like his own (which is why he was named Rosso).

Another famous example is the 1514 engraving *Melencolia* by Albrecht Dürer. Here, two angels appear looking very fed up as they survey a complex scene full of hidden meanings that have baffled art historians for centuries. Some say it represents Dürer's unhappy spiritual state of mind, whilst others believe there are cryptic clues here to Bible prophesies.

Much later, the Pre-Raphaelite group of artists painted exactly how they saw or felt things rather than in the accepted, traditional ways. Edward Burne-Jones' *Angels and the Nativity* is unique in its interpretation of the birth of Jesus. In this beautiful painting we see Mary lovingly cradling her newborn baby as Joseph kneels beside her with his back to the viewer. Three very tall, stunning angels stand silently to the left of the scene. One holds the crown of thorns, another a chalice and the third holds a jar of myrrh, all items thought of as symbols of 'the Passion', the spiritual term denoting the life and death of Jesus.

A more modern interpretation showing the connection between Earth and Heaven, and those who have to 'step up' if they want to reach salvation, is Marc Chagall's 1966 surrealist *The Jacob's Dream*. This was inspired by a vivid dream and, with his 1973 *Jacob's Ladder*, portrays angels ascending and descending a great ladder, or 'stairway to Heaven'. Some of the angels are shown as acrobats, perhaps a nod to the artist's love of the circus. To one side of the painting and carrying a lit candelabrum is a high-ranking Seraph angel.

Michelangelo di Lodovico Buonarroti Simoni, better known simply as Michelangelo, was an Italian sculptor, painter and architect in Renaissance Italy, now widely regarded as the greatest sculptor in history. One of his most famous works is the exquisite *Angel*, created in 1449 and now located at the Basilica of San Domenici, Bologna. In most respects, this marble figure is traditional, with curly hair and large wings, but unusually it is kneeling. Did Michelangelo plan it this way? He explained his work by saying, "I saw the angel in the marble and carved it until I set him free."

A very unique angel sculpture is that by William Wetmore Story, made in memory of his wife Emelyn when she died in 1894. *The Angel of Grief* represented the artist's own feelings. It shows an angel, he said, "in utter abandonment, throwing herself with drooping wings and hidden face over a funeral altar. It's what I feel. It represents prostration. Yet to do it helps me."

The largest angel sculpture in the world is *The Angel of the North*, built by Antony Gormley in Gateshead in the north-east of England, on the site of a former colliery. When Gormley was chosen as the artist for the project in 1994, many people were initially aghast, not just because of the statue itself but also because of the site and its dark memories.

"People are always asking 'why an angel?'" said Gormley. "The only response I can give is that no-one has ever seen one and we need to keep imagining them. The angel has three functions: firstly, a historic one to remind us that, below this site, coal miners worked in the dark for two hundred years; secondly, to grasp hold of the future, expressing our transition from the industrial to the information age; and lastly, to be a focus for our hopes and fears. A sculpture is an evolving thing.

"The hilltop site is important and has the feeling of being a megalithic mound. When you think of the mining that was done underneath the site, there is a poetic resonance. Men worked beneath the surface in the dark. Now in the light, there is a celebration of this industry… The effect of the piece is in the alertness, the awareness of space and the gesture of the wings, they… give a sense of embrace."

The unique and imposing *Knife Angel* literally stops people in their tracks as it's the opposite of the often beautiful and majestic angel sculptures that have been created throughout history. The statue is one of a kind, standing eight metres high and made entirely out of 100,000 seized knives collected from amnesty bins set up by more than forty police forces across the UK. It was created at the British Ironwork Centre in 2018 by the sculptor Alfie Bradley as part of the *Save a Life, Surrender Your Knife* anti-violence campaign.

The *Knife Angel's* wings are engraved with messages from families of victims of crime as a stark reminder of the tragedies caused by knife crime. Most angel statues, of course, stay where they are, but the *Knife Angel* is never still: he visits schools, churches and other venues across the nation as a blunt reminder about the danger of carrying knives.

Another poignant modern sculpture can be found in Ely's mediaeval cathedral in Cambridgeshire, England, first constructed in honour of the Virgin Mary in the 1300s. The cathedral is now home to a stunning pair of glass angel wings, at centre stage in the Lady Chapel. These iconic wings were created by glass-blower Layne Rowe who aptly named the sculpture *Solace*. The 160 blown glass feathers, nearly 50 cm long, that make up the wings were created in memory of those who lost their lives due to Covid.

Naturally, there are images of angels in architecture across the world. But we find something rather different in St. John's Cathedral at 's-Hertogenbosch, Netherlands, commonly known as Den Bosch. There are great examples of gothic architecture here and it is unique in that there are around six hundred statues adorning the building both inside and outside. Some of the statues are originals but others have been included over time. The most recent and quirky addition was sculpted in 2010 by Ton Mooy and shows an angel dressed in modern clothing, holding a mobile phone to his ear!

The stunning Lady of Reims Cathedral in France contains over two thousand sculptures, including one of the Archangel Gabriel. Yet millions of people visit the cathedral each year just to see *The Smiling Angel* statue, dating from the 13th century. This serene angel figure was positioned next to the statue of Saint Nicasius and held a palm frond denoting martyrdom, symbolically given to the saint who was murdered in the fifth century. Somehow, this palm of martyrdom has completely disappeared.

But what made *The Smiling Angel* famous was an attack on Reims during the First World War by German bombing raids. The cathedral was hit and scaffolding that was held in place for repairs caught fire; the angel was hit by a smouldering wooden beam and completely decapitated, the head breaking into more than twenty pieces. The account of this reached people right across the world as it represented the suffering of the people of France and the loss of their beloved, protective angel.

However, there is a happy ending to the story. A priest at the cathedral had the foresight to collect all the broken pieces of the decapitated statue and store them in a safe place until the war ended. Then, in 1926, she was reconstructed by the architects Max Sainsaulieu and Henri Deneux, once again smiling at all who came to see her. Not only that, but in memory of the ravages of the war, *The Smiling Angel* became the emblem of the cathedral and of the city of Reims itself.

A unique sparkling wine of the region was even created in her honour by Henri Abele, patron of the cathedral, and aptly named *Sourire Reims*, with the angel depicted on its label!

14

2
Angels today

*"Angels descending, bring from above
echoes of mercy, whispers of love."*
(Fanny J Crosby)

It is my belief through long experience that angels are pure beings of light who can help in any aspect of our lives, whether it's with change, searching for a new job or relationship, needing healing and many more situations. When we call on them, they will come to our rescue on silent wings of light. Everyone has a guardian angel that has been assigned to them from the moment they were born and our guardian loves us unconditionally, helping us throughout our lives and guiding us forward as we transcend to the afterlife. We can talk to our guardian angel with love and faith in our hearts.

The word 'angel' is derived from the Greek *angelos* which means 'messenger' and these beings appear, as we have seen, in many sacred texts. They are sometimes depicted as remote and disinterested in mundane things. This couldn't be further from the truth and angels are anything but 'fluffy'! They are highly intelligent beings, the intermediaries between Earth and the divine Source. And, as highly evolved beings, they don't experience lower emotions such as hatred, anger or jealousy as we do.

They are not human in any way, yet they can appear to us in human form so as not to frighten us. There have been many stories of angels appearing to people in times of need and in many different forms, such as helping those in danger or providing powerful guidance. We may experience this like a soft, gentle breeze or as something that's so innately profound it literally takes our breath away.

When I was a child, around the age of six, I was on my own one hot summer's day climbing up my Dad's ladder in the back yard towards a trap door. All of a sudden and without any warning, the trap door fell down and I found myself hanging by my neck with one hand holding onto the side of the ladder. However, my hand felt slippery with the heat of the sun. I was too scared to cry out and soon began to feel tired, starting to see stars. Then a stunning white light surrounded me and in an instant I felt safe and protected.

After a few moments I heard a scream and lots of shouting from the house as my Mum ran out with my Dad close behind her, their faces ghostly white. My Dad held me aloft with one hand and released the trap door with the other – just in time because I couldn't hold on any longer and he caught me as I fell. At this point, the beautiful white light I had seen disappeared, but I have never forgotten it.

The scariest thing that happened to me as an adult was when I was working on the TV show *Rescue Mediums* with my co-host Jackie. Without Archangel Michael's intervention, I may not be here now... As we were driven to the property where the unexplained paranormal activity had been occurring, I had a deep sense of foreboding. However, once we had met the homeowners, Leeanne and Willy, the feeling subsided as I warmed to this lovely down-to-earth couple. Those negative feelings came back, though, as we read our premonitions out to them and it was evident there was a very dark presence in the property. Leeanne's reactions, nodding away as we spoke, confirmed our suspicions.

At first, after the homeowners had left the property so we

could walk into each room to start our investigation, there didn't seem to be much activity at all. What didn't make sense was that our psychic drawings and premonitions seemed to lead to a very dark place, with both of us feeling that there was something bubbling under the surface. How very true this was.

Both of us felt we were being watched, or toyed with, which was unnerving as whatever, or whoever, it was obviously had no intention of showing themselves or communicating with us. At one point I felt as though someone had tripped me, nearly causing me to fall down a flight of stairs; not long afterwards, Jackie did trip on the stairs! A warning of what was to come.

When we came back to carry out the spirit rescue, we opened up our chakras (centres of spiritual energy) as usual and made sure we put psychic protection around ourselves. I always visualise wrapping myself in white light and putting on a purple cloak, a very strong spiritual colour denoting intuition and balance. As we started to fill the house with white light, we both saw a lovely spirit lady who said she was Leeanne's spirit guide who had come to help us. This was unusual. Why was it necessary, as our own spirit guides help us with our spirit rescue work? But as our respective spirit guides came in much closer than normal, we knew instantly that something unexpected was about to happen.

I felt we were being used as bait.

When it started, everything happened so quickly. I was taken completely and utterly by surprise as the dark entity overshadowed me. By this, I mean I could feel it so close around me that I started to feel dizzy, sick and absolutely petrified. Jackie's guide had told her how to contain this spirit and thankfully Leeanne's guide also came forward to help take the spirit to the light.

But just as I started to regain my composure, I realised there was another one, much stronger! The feeling hit me like a ton of bricks and I thought I was about to pass out. Not only that, it was as though this thing was trying to take over my thoughts… I could hear Jackie shouting at me but I couldn't respond. Just as I thought I couldn't hold on anymore, our guides managed to contain it.

It wasn't over yet.

By now I was so weak I was slipping in and out of consciousness, but I do remember the next entity coming forward so fast it took over my voice box completely so I couldn't speak. My mouth was moving and trembling of its own volition but, try as I might, I couldn't utter a word. I had never been so frightened in my life, and Jackie was frantically shouting at me to respond in some way. I ended up falling to the floor as the spirit showed me horrendous images that swirled in and out of my mind.

Somehow, I managed to call out inwardly to Archangel Michael for help and soon saw a pair of angel wings, calming me down. Keeping the image of the angel wings in my mind's eye, the entity shied away and as the angelic light grew brighter I felt it leave my body with a start. Again, with the help of Leeanne's guide, we sent that one over to the light too. I was a nervous wreck by this time and extremely weak, but I managed to help Jackie cleanse the rest of the house, sending a big thank you to Archangel Michael for getting me out of a really dangerous situation.

After having a psychic reading with me, Jane told me how the angels had responded to her even though she was very doubtful. Jane lived in a large finca with six dogs, several stray cats and an aviary full of rescued birds. The message I'd received was that a Galgo dog (a Spanish greyhound) would come into her life but straight away Jane said that would never happen, they weren't her type of dog at all even though she had an overwhelming feeling to look for a rescue dog and had much love to give. I was adamant because the angels kept repeating it.

For several months she searched on numerous websites until she saw a puppy she was drawn to. She arranged to visit but the day before received a phone call to say that the puppy had disappeared. The people felt that someone had stolen her. On the other hand, they had another puppy that they wanted to "get rid of" and sent a photo and video of her.

On the film, this young dog's head was lowered and Jane could see fear in her eyes. She knew instantly she had to go and see her. With a friend she drove to Cartagena, pulled off the road and arrived at a small stone house on a campo. There was furniture stacked untidily outside the property and filth and rubbish everywhere. When the puppy was brought out it was yelping in fear, panic stricken, struggling to get free and then running for cover under the furniture.

Jane knew she couldn't leave her in this house so picked her up very gently, expecting her to cry, but she simply lay quietly in Jane's arms without moving. They couldn't get out of there fast enough and, back at home, the puppy was introduced to the other dogs and soon settled down happily. And yes, it was a Galgo!

Jacky Newcomb is a well-known 'angel lady' and author who has appeared on television several times over the years. She told me that she is happy for me to share some of her experiences.[1]

When one of her daughters was small she was suffering from a bad stomach virus and her mother was running around exhausted by cleaning up, and running out of fresh linen and towels. She even made her daughter a makeshift bed on the bathroom floor, but still had to run in to help her frequently. When she eventually threw herself onto her bed to rest, she again heard her daughter calling for her. As she dragged herself to the bathroom half asleep, she saw the girl pale and sweating with so much pain on her face that Jacky felt close to breaking point.

"Angels, where are you when I need you?" she shouted. "I just can't do this anymore so please help my daughter by taking over."

Immediately, she heard what she describes as beautiful orchestral music which at first she thought must be coming from some event outside. But who would be playing angelic music in the early hours of the morning? Perhaps it was a television that had been left on in the house? She checked and the televisions were turned off. She opened a window to look outside but couldn't see or hear anything. Frustrated, and beside herself with worry and tiredness she closed the window, realising that the music was actually inside the bathroom!

---

[1] *An Angel Treasury,* Jacky Newcomb (HarperCollins, 2011)

And suddenly she felt peace washing over her as the music softened and saw that her daughter had gone quiet and fallen fast asleep. The music then faded away and Jacky crept out of the bathroom and into her own bed, falling fast asleep. The next morning, her daughter was completely free of the virus and Jacky thanked the host of angels for their unique yet magnificent answer to her plea for help.

Another amazing account was shared by Jacky's friend. One night as she lay asleep in bed, her young daughter turned over and was about to roll out onto the hard floor. Waking up with a start, she was more than a little surprised to find herself being quickly but gently lifted up into the air and back over the bed by unseen arms. She couldn't see anyone but didn't feel frightened.

Then she saw her younger sister standing by the bedroom door staring at her. No words were exchanged and the girl then felt herself being slowly lowered onto the bed, whereupon she promptly went back to sleep. The next morning she assumed it had all been a vivid dream, yet at breakfast her younger sister said, "I heard a noise last night coming from your bedroom so I came to see if you were alright, and you were floating above your bed."

Bonni lives in Canada and tells a story of when she had retired from driving a school bus and started a new job driving adults with learning difficulties to a day centre where there were social activities for them. This also allowed their caregivers some respite.

"I loved my work," she says, "and invoked my angels every day to see us through our snow storms and keep my clients calm and safe."

Her little bus had more than a few quirks, though, that would cause her to shimmy along the road with a few clunking and creaking noises. She asked her boss to get the bus checked over but he always dismissed her concerns. It was just an old bus, the wheelchair lift just needed some oil, everything was fine. Bonni still had her doubts but assumed he knew what he was talking about.

One day, all her clients had been safely delivered to the day centre and Bonni was on her way to a nearby town. 'Something', she says, made her decide to stay off the highway and choose a quiet country road instead. Suddenly, as she turned a corner, she heard the rear of the bus making ungodly noises and then "all heck broke loose!" as the vehicle veered and jerked and Bonni fought to keep it on the road. It came to a stop on the shoulder of the road and she laid her forehead onto the steering wheel, saying a prayer of thanks to the angels.

But the drama wasn't over yet.

Looking to one side through the large windows she was astonished to see the two rear wheels rolling past... the axle had ground itself into the soft shoulder of the road and both wheels, clearly loose, had flown off. So that's what all the clunking noises had been!

She watched helplessly as they gained momentum and bounced a little higher each time they hit the road, shooting away ahead... straight towards a van turning out of a driveway and facing the bus. Bonni could see the driver's eyes widen as he realised what was about to happen. Instinctively, Bonni prayed, "Oh, no! Angels, please help."

One of the wheels slowed, wobbled and then flopped harmlessly onto its side in the ditch. "Thank you, angels." But the second wheel kept going right towards the van and the driver wrapped his arms around his head and ducked down below the dashboard. The wheel made one more bounce, launching it towards the windshield and then, just a few feet away... made a sudden sharp turn to the side, disappearing into the ditch as if a giant hand had come down and given it a push.

Even that wasn't the most amazing thing about the whole experience.

The van driver jumped out and ran towards Bonni in her wrecked bus, saying he didn't understand how she'd managed to keep it from flipping over. Then while Bonni called her boss to arrange for a tow truck, she noticed that the man was climbing around inside the bus.

"Where's that other guy?" he kept saying.

"What other guy?" Bonni asked. "I'm alone."

"No," he laughed, "while you were bringing this bus to a halt, I saw a big man bent over behind your seat with his arms around yours. He was helping you to control the bus. He was huge, wearing a big purple ski jacket."

"Thank you, Archangel Michael!" Bonni breathed.

Rolf had never believed in angels until one extraordinary night. His wife was fighting cancer in a hospice and he was allowed to stay with her overnight with a bed next to hers. One night he awoke to see two angels standing over her. He said they were very large and looked male, like warriors. He rubbed his eyes thinking he was seeing things but they were definitely there.

"Please don't take her now," he said out loud, turning his head to the wall as he didn't want to see her go. When he turned back to look at her, there was just one angel at her side with the other one was standing right next to Rolf.

The next day, his wife woke up and said she would like to go out for a while so he took her near their home and she gasped in happiness as he pushed her wheelchair around her favourite place. She adored nature and her face lit up, seeing the trees, butterflies and flowers and listening to the birdsong with a smile on her face. Then Rolf realised the pain that had distorted her face for so long had disappeared.

That evening, he took her back to the hospice where, for the first time, she said she didn't need any morphine as she couldn't feel any pain. She passed away peacefully in her sleep that night.

As I said earlier, sometimes angels appear to us in human form. Sandy tells the strange story of someone she met on the train when she was going to work as a legal secretary. She was also going to night school two evenings a week taking legal courses and had her large, heavy books with her in her husband's hockey bag. On the very crowded express train none of the morning commuters appreciated this huge bag taking up most of the foot room, and many of them were scowling at her and making comments.

Then Sandy saw an older lady sitting to her right. She hadn't noticed her before but she was smiling and quietly asked what Sandy was studying. She told the lady that litigation was her worst subject and she was very nervous about a test she had to do that night. Suddenly it seemed as though a hush came over the train as the woman quietly told Sandy that she would do very well and indeed change law firms to work as a legal clerk. She was very encouraging and sweet, and spoke as though she knew and cared about Sandy.

When the train pulled into the station, people let Sandy get off first because of her large bag and she waited on the platform to thank the lady, but she didn't get off the train. There was only one exit door in that part of the train but the lady seemed to have completely vanished. Sandy felt goose bumps and lightheaded.

Everything the woman had said came true, and Sandy is convinced she was her guardian angel.

Speaking of guardian angels, Pamela sent me an extraordinary message. She had been going through a particularly stressful time and sent out a prayer asking her guardian angel for a sign that they were watching over her. The next day she was at a charity fair where she bought a tombola ticket that won a prize, a beautiful red satin box.

Opening the box she found a beautiful crystal angel with a note attached, reading, 'I am your guardian angel and I am always with you.' That was enough proof for Pamela.

There are many such stories of angels coming forward to help us. Angelina describes how angels saved her life when she was sixteen years-old.

"I was following my friend across the road and forgot to look both ways. My friend screamed and I turned to see a white car was coming really fast straight towards me. I froze on the spot. Then the next thing I remember was being back on the side of the road. My friend said that I'd made a weird kind of jump up and backwards. I know I didn't do it because I was too frightened to move. Since then, I have always believed in angels."

An especially dramatic and evidential account was given by two young boys, about eleven years-old, when they were being checked over in hospital following an accident. They had been playing at what they called their "secret place", which was a river at a wooded area not far from their homes. They said they called it that because all the times they had played there they had never seen anyone else.

Boys being boys, they were seeing who could dive into the murky river the deepest. They said they knew there were long reeds in the river but weren't scared because they'd swum there many times before; this time they had a bet on who could dive the deepest. The first boy dived in and almost immediately his friend heard him shouting for help as he'd got caught up in the reeds and couldn't move. So then the other boy jumped in and tried to free him but he got stuck as well. They both thought they were going to drown.

They shouted out for help even though they knew there'd be no-one around to hear them, but what happened next was quite incredible. The boys saw a bright white light glowing around the reeds under the water and felt themselves being lifted up together into the air then gently put down on the ground. Wondering what on earth had happened, they looked around and saw a strange man.

"He had a face like a lovely woman," one of the boys said, "with golden hair. And he wore what looked like a woman's white blouse and white baggy trousers. I think I've seen pictures of him before at school but I can't remember where. And we could see he had white flowers in his hand – like the lilies my Mum buys. Oh, then he shouted, 'Peace be with you, boys' and walked away behind the trees. We didn't see him again. A few minutes later, my parents arrived and brought us here."

The boys didn't know, of course, that the senior nurse they were telling their story to was Glynis Amy Allen, an hereditary medium. She has since written several books describing her experiences working alongside spirit doctors and angels.[2]

---

[2] *The Angels Beside Us*, Glynis Amy Allen (Local Legend, 2020)

One thing that puzzled Glynis about the boy's story was how his Mum and Dad knew where they were. His mother said she kept hearing a voice from 'somewhere' saying, "Wildwood. You have to go, your son is in danger." So she got all the family and neighbours together to search for them.

Glynis is convinced that the man who saved the boys' lives was Archangel Gabriel. Throughout history, he has been known to have special care for children and is also the elemental angel of water. He brings a white ray of light and is often depicted holding white lilies as a symbol of peace. And actually, this beautiful angel can be seen as male or female, just as the boys described.

Working in a busy hospital, Glynis also shares this breathtaking story about a young woman in her care who was dying from advanced lung cancer. As Glynis sat beside her bed she noticed how often the young woman would face the wall and ask things like, "Am I going to die tonight?" Who was she talking to? The young woman smiled and said that she saw the faces of angels there – and they answered her questions honestly. Then she suddenly sat bolt upright.

"There is an angel right behind you now. Don't move," she said, grabbing Glynis' hand to stop her turning around. Glynis could smell the fragrance of white roses, feeling a powerful presence nearby as her patient's face glowed with her eyes shining brightly. Glynis then turned to see a huge angelic being with white hair and deep blue eyes full of love.

"Nurse, I know why he is here," said the young woman, "and I don't want any more medication now. I just want you to hold my hand because I am going to see my little girl and my Mum very soon. Can you help me into my pink nightdress with the teddies on it, please, so my daughter will recognise me?"

Clearly, she knew she wasn't long for this world and was preparing herself. Glynis helped her into her favourite nightdress and made sure she was comfortable, holding her cold hand as she slipped away peacefully. Soon afterwards, as Glynis and another nurse were carrying out the last offices, the scent of white roses came again and both nurses heard a whooshing sound as the young woman's soul transitioned safely.

Sometimes, it seems that children are more easily able than adults to be aware of the angels around us, perhaps because they haven't yet learned to doubt such things. Carla tells that very soon after her best friend had died, her five year-old daughter crawled into her bed in the early morning. Carla was still sleepy and had her eyes shut as the girl chatted.

"Why is there an angel going into your bathroom?" she asked suddenly. Carla opened her eyes instantly but saw nothing, so she asked her daughter what the angel looked like. She said she wore a purple dress and had wings "as big as Daddy" and long dark hair, but she didn't walk like us and was "kind of floating". The angel had stopped beside Carla's dresser where there was a fabric angel she had bought from a craft show. When they got up to look she had disappeared as quickly as she had arrived, but the experience gave Carla great comfort.

Sometimes we can experience that without actually seeing anything. Linda says that she lost her business partner to brain cancer a while ago and, "She was the closest thing there could be to an angel walking on the Earth. She was a gifted psychic medium and someone who always loved helping others."

A few weeks after her passing, Linda was still feeling raw grief when suddenly one day she felt the strong energy of someone nearby. It stopped her in her tracks, she says, and she was literally buzzing with energy.

"I knew it was her as I could feel her loving vibration and I didn't want it to end, or the blue light that accompanied her. I knew in that instant that the angels had sent her to me, to let me know she was okay. Even though I have lost a soul sister and cherished friend, I know I have gained a powerful angelic ally in spirit."

A simple belief in the angels and a quiet prayer can be all that is needed to draw in their loving and protective energy – and even turn our lives around. Carmen's mother, her best friend, passed away when she was a teenager and she felt totally bereft, lost and afraid. She told me that she'd gone into meltdown, not knowing how to deal with her feelings or where to turn. When her father met another woman who treated Carmen badly, she turned to drink. And when her father also passed away, Carmen really hit the skids by using drugs and completely going 'off the rails'.

Her mental health was suffering badly and she started hearing a voice in her head, telling her she was rubbish and wouldn't amount to anything. She thought she was going mad. And even though she got herself off the alcohol and drugs and married her loving partner, she still heard that negative voice.

She told me that it was only when she met me and started following my Facebook page, *Discover the Angels*, everything began to change. She started praying to the angels and sharing her pain with them, something she had never been able to do with anyone on Earth. The negative voice stopped, she became happy in her own skin and has since built up a successful business.

As we see from all of these true stories, the angels can literally come to our rescue.

3
Bringing in the light

"An angel brings lightness of spirit into your life."
(The author)

As a child, I was totally alone with a gift I didn't understand, assuming that everyone could experience the same as me. It didn't take long to learn that this was not the case, which meant I had no-one I could talk to or go to for answers. I had one sister and we had strict parents. In school I was referred to as 'Alice in Wonderland' by teachers and pupils alike because I would often drift off into my own imaginary world. I preferred it there. I even used to sleepwalk a lot and talk in my sleep. Yes, all in all I was an odd child but I didn't know why.

Yet in times of turmoil or darkness, I always somehow knew that there was something or someone else out there looking after me. I can only describe this as a deep inner feeling that I would always be looked after, even though I didn't know by whom. This sense was so strong that I never questioned it, despite having no tangible proof that another realm existed apart from the Earth. I just had total belief in my heart that it did. And as I grew up, I strove to find out the truth of it all.

As a small child, I often felt scared in my bedroom because I could hear whispering and unexplained noises such as footsteps and bangs. But I couldn't see anyone there so I pulled the blanket over my head and after a while the noises would stop and everything went deathly quiet.

At this point one particular night, I could see a light that was so bright it was penetrating through the blanket. Thinking my Mum had come into the room silently and turned on the light, I pulled the blanket away and sat up. That was when I saw the whole room lit up by a stunning white light that began to move and change into smaller gold and silver lights in the shape of blobs like those inside a lava lamp.

Instead of feeling frightened, I felt comforted and happy as I watched the silver and golden shapes dancing around and getting brighter by the minute. Eventually I started to feel really tired so I lay down watching the moving blobs until I fell asleep. When I woke up the next morning they had gone, but now I knew that there were other beings around me that I could talk to and ask for help whenever I felt alone or scared. Even at such an early age, I felt I didn't have to see the angels to believe in them.

School was difficult for me and my Mum has told me many times about the very first day she took me to primary school. It was about a fifteen minute walk from our house; once she had dropped me off, she waved goodbye and went home. Not long afterwards she heard a knock at the front door and opened it to find me standing there.

"I don't like school and I'm not going back," I announced.

Of course, she promptly marched me back to school. The teacher told her that the gate was securely locked, there was a high wall all around the site, and neither she nor my Mum could understand how I got out. I don't remember – how did I escape?

My Mum often reminds me that I was "a strange child"! For example, I always knew what the gifts were in the presents that she and Dad had wrapped up when it was my birthday or for Christmas. What she didn't know is that I was being told in my mind by a lovely gentle voice what was inside each one. In an attempt to fool me, my parents used to disguise presents by putting them in different sized boxes, but I still always knew what they all were. So they gave up in the end and resigned themselves to the fact that I was 'different'.

However, they never spoke of my gift and I gave up trying to talk to them about it. Later in life, I asked my Mum why she or Dad didn't speak to me about how I seemed to know things that others didn't.

"We didn't want you to think you were any different to other children," was her response. But the fact of the matter is that I was different – and I still am. It didn't help that neither of them believed in otherworldly beings so I realised it was impossible for me to talk to them about the moving blobs and the sometimes scarier beings in my room.

One of my earliest experiences of physically seeing what I would describe as a 'child angel' was when I was around seven years-old. In the playground at junior school I spotted a little boy I had never seen before. He was dressed in strange clothes and was looking directly at me with a sad expression on his face. I felt drawn to him so went over to talk to him. The conversation seemed to be within my mind rather than verbally, but I didn't think this was in any way odd at the time.

When the bell rang for us to go back into school, all the children started to walk towards the building but the little boy just stood there. I called him over and asked which class he was in, but he remained rooted to the spot and said nothing. So I ran to catch up with my best friend and asked her who the new boy was; she didn't know what I was talking about and when I pointed to him she said there was nobody there.

I could still see him quite distinctly and didn't understand how she couldn't. Very puzzled, I turned back to ask him again who he was, and gasped as there was now the biggest bright white light all around him in the shape of angel wings. He smiled at me, waved and simply disappeared. When I told my friend this later, she said I was stupid and was making things up. She even went on to tell the other children in our class what I'd said, resulting in me being bullied from that day forward. (Needless to say, she wasn't my best friend anymore!)

After this incident I learned very quickly to keep what I could see and sense to myself, realising that other people do not see or talk to otherworldly beings. I have often wondered about that boy, though, and will never forget the serene smile on his face as those wings of light surrounded him. Was he an earthbound spirit that I somehow sent to the light? Was he a child angel? Perhaps he came to reassure me that my sense of other realms was true.

As I've said, angels and spirit have always been around me from as far back as I can remember. I could always see or feel 'extras' in the room and at first assumed that everyone else could too. However, so as not to be bullied or laughed at, I kept my otherworldly experiences to myself. It was difficult, not being able to share my experiences and fears with anyone else.

On the other hand, it was the angels themselves who came forward to help me. One was the young boy described above, and then there was my encounter with a pretty winged figure in my bedroom, dressed all in pink. She would appear whenever I cried out and was scared, especially at night when I felt and saw spirit people in my room. She made me feel comforted and often sang to me. At first I called her 'the pink lady', which made her smile.

Gradually, I became aware that she was a guardian angel who was always with me. I always had an image of her dressed in pink with a vibrant light around her and, of course, a loving smile. Every time I have gone through a difficult time in my life, I have asked her for help and known without a doubt that she was there. It has felt so good to be protected by such a beautiful divine energy.

With the passing years, I began to understand the messages she gave me through my dreams and meditation. Then finally came the most wonderful moment when I was in my spiritual haven at home and I saw a flash of pink light. There she was, as radiant as ever, gliding towards me. I had never actually seen her so clearly before so I was blown away and very happy. Then she gave me her name, Mya, before leaving in a flash.

Although I know she loves me unconditionally, and tries to guide me, I haven't always gone down the right paths in life. In fact, I have very often hurtled down the wrong ones. In moments of reflection, I have a vision of her with a cigarette in one hand and a brandy in the other, slumped forward with her head in her hands in total despair!

As I grew up, life was often challenging on so many levels, especially because I was able to communicate with angelic and spiritual beings but didn't understand how to assimilate what was real to me and not to others. Thankfully, this changed once I had been taught how to protect my energy field at a local psychic development group, as well as how to close down our chakras so we're not open to any and every kind of energy all the time. This really was a breakthrough for me! I then went on to learn more about the angels through my own experience, and by research and attending courses such as Angel Harmonic Healing, Angel Magic and Angelic Reiki.

I cannot now imagine a life without the angels beside me, as they have helped me cope through the most challenging times such as breakdown of relationships and the loss of human and furry loved ones to the afterlife. And of course, they protect me in my work as a rescue medium…

I called at the small flat in the local village on my own at first as I can ascertain pretty quickly whether there's a stuck, or earthbound, spirit that's causing unexplained paranormal activity or if it's just a build-up of negative human energy, perhaps due to arguments in the home or some form of psychic attack. This time, I knew straight away that a spirit was causing havoc and it needed to be dealt with expeditiously.

As soon as the homeowner opened the door and I walked into the small flat, intense energy seemed to swirl all around me and I felt as though I was walking through treacle and not getting anywhere fast. Whatever was there was strong, with an undercurrent of panic to the point of hysteria. I didn't want to frighten the homeowners so I kept these feelings to myself, but told them I had detected something there to confirm what they had already experienced. Together with my trusted team of helpers, we would do everything we could to help them.

This young couple and their cat had only recently moved into their new home and from day one had experienced a plethora of negative energy, such as deep cold spots in the living room, items being moved about noisily and being touched by cold unseen hands. They were also bewildered by their cat's reaction to its new home. He was so scared on the first day they entered that he wouldn't come out of his crate. Apparently, the only time he did come out was when a treat was offered, but even then he would approach cautiously, stare at a certain area on the wall, then growl and run back into his crate, shaking.

The unexplained activity got stronger in the flat and the final straw came when the young man was brushing his teeth in the bathroom one evening. He said he felt a deep cold surrounding him and, as he looked up at his own image in the mirror, he clearly saw a ghostly female figure standing behind him. He described her as having long straggly hair with a distraught look on her face. She held her arms out to him then disappeared.

Soon my trusted team and I arrived at the flat. We asked the homeowners to leave while we carried out what would hopefully be a normal and successful spirit rescue. But as soon as we entered the premises, all of us felt a strong, dense energy like thick fog. The little cat in his crate stared at us with saucer eyes and we all felt for him, pressed to the back of the crate and very subdued.

Usually with a spirit rescue it can take a long time before the spirit is ready to communicate, but not this one! It all happened very fast. All of a sudden I felt as though someone had walked through me and I nearly keeled over. Then I felt a jolt as the spirit actually came into my body. Yes, it was a female entity who felt utterly bereft and desperate, to the point where I had to rush into the bathroom with one of my team members holding my hair back as I was physically sick. I then had the most horrendous stomach pain and realised the woman had been pregnant.

"My baby, where is my baby?" I heard her say.

She was becoming delirious now and the physical conditions she was putting on me were getting more difficult to bear. I was becoming weaker but knew I had to keep hold of her energy so I could find out what her story was and why she was stuck between two worlds. At this point I sent up a silent prayer to Archangel Gabriel, the angel of women and children, to help us send the distraught spirit to the light.

While I was being overshadowed, my two team members did an amazing job asking her salient questions in a cool and calm manner in order to gain her trust. When her story was revealed through me, it was heartbreaking.

At her time of death, she had been a young girl around sixteen years of age and was very scared. What she had endured during her short life had been kept a secret as she said no-one would have believed her if she had told them. Her parents had died when she was very young and her uncle, a priest, took her in. But she was petrified of him and we reeled in horror as she relived how he had raped her consistently until at last she was carrying his baby. She knew she would be vilified and cast out of the village as no-one would believe the child she was carrying was the priest's.

She felt she had no alternative than to run and hide. And I felt all of her emotions as she realised she was going to die, totally alone and unloved, giving birth to her stillborn baby in scrubland on the edge of the village.

Back in the room, I felt the energy change and saw movement in front of me. It was a beautiful, bright white ray of light within which a large angel stepped forward. Archangel Gabriel had heard me! The angel told me to connect with the female spirit for the last time. I did so and felt her becoming much calmer as she too had seen the large angel in the room. Everything happened so quickly at this point as she left me and walked towards Archangel Gabriel.

My colleagues told me later that at this point I shouted out, "The bells, the bells!", and a moment later the actual bells in the village church peeled three times. The young woman opened her arms and another angel stepped forward saying, "I am Archangel Azrael, here to guide this beautiful soul safely to the afterlife." Then I watched the spirit, a beautiful gleaming light all around her, appear to walk through the wall with Gabriel on one side and Azrael on the other. And the door to the other side was sealed.

This was such an intense rescue that it took me a while to come round. When I did, my team members told me that as the spirit was recalling through me the horror of losing her baby, the cat started running around like a mad thing. Then just as the angels were guiding her towards the light, the cat came and sat calmly beside me as if to say, "Good job!"

All of us were relieved that the heavy energy that had permeated the flat had now lifted and we thanked the angels for helping to bring peace to the female spirit as well as for the homeowners. The cat was now trotting around with his tail in the air and winding himself round our legs. We gave him some food and afterwards he sat down, giving himself a good wash with a contented look on his face. This was, after all, his home and he was finally happy to be here.

During the terrible Covid pandemic that caused suffering and devastation for millions of people across the world, many people reached out to me to ask which angels they should call on to help them with mental health problems, with the grief of losing loved ones, with no longer having a job and much more. During that time I did online readings and posted free YouTube videos on grounding, alignment and meditation. I also wrote poems and prayers that had been channelled by the angels as well as posting beautiful images, quotations and affirmations on social media.

People asked for help with specific problems such as abuse, loneliness and despair, and with understanding how to strengthen their intuitive instincts or protect themselves against negative energy. This was something I could do, reaching out to as many people as possible with the love and guidance of the angels.

One thing I couldn't do during lockdown, of course, was in person spirit rescue. So the angels and my spirit team helped me to send earthbound spirits to the light remotely, helping people in isolation with 'unwanted guests' from the spirit world who created unexplained negative activity in their homes.

One woman asked for my help because she felt her family were under attack by a dark figure, a male energy that was creating a lot of unpleasant activity in the home, mostly centred around her two year-old granddaughter. After connecting with her remotely I realised that, whilst their home wasn't haunted as such, they were under immense psychic attack. This is something that can happen when other people simply project negative and hurtful thoughts such as jealousy and anger. If the person on the receiving end is particularly sensitive, this can cause mayhem in many ways, from experiencing mental health problems to feeling as though their home is haunted.

If you are under psychic attack, or if a ghost is present in the house that you are concerned about, you would in normal circumstances ask a reputable medium with spirit rescue experience to deal with the situation on your behalf. The best thing to do is to cleanse and bless the house during a personal visit; but I wasn't allowed to travel so had to do it virtually in order to help her.

In such cases, I would ask Archangel Michael to guide and protect me and others involved. I believe he is the best angel to call on for help as he is known to be the angel that helps against spirit attachment and psychic attack. During lockdown, the angels and my spirit guides pulled out all the stops to help those in turmoil. I didn't have to wait too long to find out that the work was going on because I started to have many vivid, lucid dreams in which I was assisting the angels with spirit rescues. Then in the morning, I would wake up with my heart thumping as though I'd just come back into my body.

There was also one moment when the angels gave me a clear instruction… I had been sitting up in bed reading when, just as I reached for a glass of water, I saw a figure moving quickly round the side of the bed, past the mirror and the wardrobe. It appeared to be floating and was the height of a child, dressed all in white with a glow around it.

"Who the hell is that?" I shouted out in my usual refined way, and it disappeared. Yet I was literally tingling from the top of my head to my toes. I recognised that feeling instantly as it reminded me of how I tingle when my pink guardian angel comes close and I see her gliding across the floor. In that moment I felt blessed and I thanked the angel for visiting me.

Then, when I woke up in the morning, it was like a rocket had gone off inside me. A real light-bulb moment. I was being told in no uncertain terms to write a book about the angels! This made sense. After all, why not share the love of the angels with you? Everyone deserves a little divine magic in their lives.

4
Communicating with the angels

"The angels are waiting for your call."
(The author)

As an angel tutor, I believe that our first port of call when connecting with the angelic realm is our own guardian angel, who has accompanied us personally from the moment we were born and will remain with us until we transcend to the spirit world. I hope you will want to take a step closer to communicating with your angel, your closest companion. Who else will know everything about us (even if we may not want them to!) and understand everything that we are experiencing? Whether we are just starting out, wanting to know more about the angels, or have already seen, felt or sensed them around us, we can all learn to communicate better with them.

In my experience, our guardian angels work telepathically through us, in our thoughts or dreams. For example, if you are worried, scared or anxious, it's good to talk to your angel and ask for their help. They will often send confirmation that they have heard these prayers, such as with a sign or omen, a synchronicity. If you think you have already received a sign from your guardian angel, and believe without a doubt that they have paid you a visit, think about how you knew this.

There should be a deep sense of knowing, a gut feeling telling you that it is authentic.

One of the best ways to connect to your angel is through meditation, either by working with an angel tutor or by listening to some of the many guided meditations online. As with anything else, practice is the key. And as you start to receive messages in response, you will gain the confidence to find out more. Try to be patient as this relationship will develop with divine timing. We will receive what we need to know when we are able to recognise and understand it – and the angels know more about this than perhaps we do.

Suppose you want to ask your angel specific questions, such as their name, it's important to start by choosing a good place and time to connect with them. This could be somewhere peaceful in your home where you know you will not be disturbed, or you may feel closer to them in the open air such as at the beach or in a beautiful park full of trees, flowers and plants.

If you're in your home, do whatever feels right to you such as lighting candles on an angel altar if you have one, burning aromatherapy oil or listening to soft and gentle music. In an outside space, Mother Nature will share all the sounds you will need, such as the ebb and flow of the sea, the sound of birds singing or the rustling of leaves on the trees.

Once you are comfortable, do a grounding ritual to help you feel balanced, happy and at peace. For example, you could visualise roots like those of a tree connecting deep within the earth and bringing white light up through the soles of your feet and through the rest of your body to fill it with divine white light.

Concentrate on your breath and practise slowing it down. A simple exercise is to take a deep breath in, hold for a count of three and then, as you exhale, visualise letting go of anything that no longer serves you. Repeat this as often as you wish, with patience, and feel yourself relaxing. One of the best ways to finish your grounding is to see yourself in a bubble of rainbow light or to surround yourself in golden light. But there really is no right or wrong here, your angel will be happy with whatever you choose to do.

Once everything feels right to you, you can start to talk to your guardian angel as you would to a good friend. You can begin the conversation by thanking them for being by your side and perhaps asking them to send you a sign as confirmation that they can hear you. Some people like to say a short incantation out loud to help make a stronger connection with your angel. You can choose your own words, or say something like,

> *"Guardian angel by my side,*
> *please say your name and always guide*
> *with the shining light of the Divine.*
> *I thank you dearly for being mine."*

Please don't worry if nothing seems to happen straight away, just trust that a name will present itself to you when the moment is right. This could be given in many ways, with a sign you notice, a thought that just comes into your head or within a beautiful dream.

Once you have started practising connecting with your angel and trusting in their love and guidance, there is no reason why you shouldn't feel or sense them around you. Of course, to actually see an angel is quite rare, but it can happen as they are able to show themselves to us in any way they wish or that seems appropriate. However, for the most part, angels will appear in visions such as during meditation or by entering our dreams. During sleep we are on a subconscious state of mind where our body and brain have slowed down and relaxed, which makes it easier for the angels to step in and communicate with us.

So if we ask our guardian angel a question before going to sleep, and then remember a dream that is salient when we wake up, we can know that all is well and we have made a good connection. What if we have difficulty in sleeping? Then why not say a prayer to your guardian angel, such as,

*"Dear guardian angel, please help me to rest well,
bless my dreams and keep me safe this night.
Let me feel your presence beside me
with the purest love and light. Thank you."*

Suppose, then, that we have asked our angel for a sign to let us know that they have heard our prayers. From now on we must trust in their presence and practise a mindful attitude, being 'in the moment', so we can recognise the signs they leave for us. What kind of signs could they give?

A synchronicity is an extraordinary and meaningful thing that happens at a special moment in time or in a special place. So some signs will be tangible, such as a feather, usually white, where we would not expect to see one, or perhaps a particular bird or butterfly coming very close to us just as we are thinking about or talking with the angels. Other signs could be seeing special numbers repeatedly, finding a coin in an unusual place (known as 'pennies from Heaven') or even seeing incandescent lights before us, particularly in white, gold or silver as these are the highest vibrational colours of the angelic realm.

Another beautiful way the angels can communicate with us is through music, such as hearing the most uplifting choral voices when neither the television nor the radio are turned on. There may be an unusual temperature change, such as a lovely warm breeze that surrounds us even on a cold day. And then there is a sudden euphoric feeling of knowing exactly what to do, as the answer to our prayer pops into our head as if by magic.

Some of these signs are quite common, but there will often be others that appear in a very unique way and be personal just for us. It could be something seen, heard or even smelled, such as the aroma of a particular flower or a scent that we recognise as having a special meaning for us. When these things happen, we should always go with how we feel at the time. If we sense with every fibre of our being that we have been visited by an angel, then our intuition is telling us without any doubt that this is true.

One of the most unusual signs I have received from the angels happened not long after we had moved, for health reasons, to our new home. I was wondering if we had done the right thing, moving hook line and sinker to a new country. We didn't know anyone and I would have to start from scratch to build up my spiritual practice. I did feel that we had made the right decision but doubts did keep creeping into my mind from time to time.

What helped me to feel more at home was enjoying creating a magical haven in what was to become my healing room for potential new clients. So I asked the angels to bless the space as I drew Reiki symbols around the room and set up a brand new angel altar upon which I placed angel figurines, crystals and candles.

When the room was ready I sat down to communicate with the angels, asking them for a sign that we would be happy as residents in our new home and country, and that they would guide people to me for readings and healing treatments. I thanked them for listening to me and then stepped outside the house onto the patio area. There, on one of the chairs, was a large red balloon in the shape of a heart! It was a beautiful, sunny spring day with no breeze at all, and there were no children in our community. I gave a big thank you to the angels because this could only have come as a welcome sign of love from them.

Our new life was happy but there came a point when I was feeling that my spiritual practice had been making slow progress for a while; I wanted to know that things would move forward with new ideas. So on one particular morning, I asked the angels for a definitive sign. Well, I didn't have to wait long for their answer as it came that very afternoon.

I was having coffee with my husband and a friend at a busy beach bar, having a few laughs and enjoying one another's company in the warm autumn sunshine. After we'd asked for the bill, I stood up to leave and saw something glinting on my chair. At first, I thought it was a bit of gold paper, like the foil in a cigarette packet, but when I looked again I realised that the object was solid. I picked it up.

It was a perfect, golden angel pendant set with beautiful stones. My husband and friend had never seen anything like this before and couldn't believe their eyes. There was certainly nothing on the chair when I'd sat down. Of all the chairs at all the cafés on that very busy day, the angel pendant appeared on my chair just after I had asked the angels for a reassuring sign. This was truly magical, a genuine apport – an object that materialises in the presence of a medium, a very rare event. Definitely a 'wow' moment!

It turns out that I'm not the only one to receive balloons from the angels… Peter is a medium and he told me he often gets this kind of sign when he asks the angels an important question or needs some reassurance. One morning he'd been deep in thought regarding an awful situation that was happening in his life. He asked the angels for a sign that things would get resolved in the right way.

Literally a few minutes later, he heard a noise at the front door and went to open it. There on his doormat was a green balloon! It would have needed to travel over a high brick wall, against the prevailing wind, passing roses and a huge bougainvillea both full of prickly thorns to get where it had landed. Peter said that even as a medium he was blown away by the effort the angels had made to put his mind at rest.

The medium Glynis also tells of the very unusual way in which she knows when the angels are with her. She loves to make dolls and uses different coloured buttons for their faces and on their clothes. However, over the years when she has asked the angels for help with a particular issue she has often then found specific coloured buttons, even in teacups and the dogs' beds.

The buttons even seem to travel too… Glynis had prayed to Archangel Jophiel, who brings a yellow ray of light when she comes near, for help with healing a lady who had asked for help. The following day the lady phoned Glynis to say she had found a yellow button on her saucer!

One of the most wonderful and important ways in which the

angels show their love is when we are grieving someone's loss and feeling very alone. Carol tells what happened when her husband was seriously ill and eventually passed away.

"My husband Barry suffered for years with a genetic disease. He was in hospital for an operation on his gall bladder. But his heart was failing and I was so worried he wouldn't recover from an operation like that. Sure enough, the next day I received the call that anyone would dread, to say that Barry had passed away.

"The next day I went to the funeral home with my friend to make arrangements and as we were leaving we passed a heather bush. I couldn't believe it when twenty or more red admiral butterflies lifted off the bush and completely surrounded my body, circling me from my head to my feet. My friend said afterwards that she couldn't see me for the butterflies! Red admirals were Barry's favourite butterfly so I knew it was a sign from the angels to tell me that he was now free of any pain in the spirit world."

Earlier I mentioned the rare sign from the angels of 'pennies from Heaven'. Carol told me of her experience after she had lost her beloved daughter, Rakel, due to aggressive lupus and vasculitis which she had suffered from for seventeen years before she passed away. On the day of the funeral, Carol prayed hard to the angels for support and peace as there had been a family dispute and she was worried about seeing certain family members at the service. In the event, everything went to plan and Carol was able to say goodbye to her beloved daughter.

Later, at home, she was relaxing when she heard a strange sound from above. She looked up and watched in awe as small coins suddenly began to drop from the ceiling! She knew it was a sign from the angels but wasn't sure what it meant, so she added the coins up and it came to exactly seventeen pence. She thanked the angels for such a clear sign to confirm that they had guided Rakel safely over to the afterlife and that she was now at peace.

The angels are androgynous and can appear to us as masculine or feminine even though some, particularly the archangels, have usually been described as male in traditional religions. Archangel Gabriel for example, can appear to many as masculine, yet has feminine qualities due to being the angel with particular care for women and children, and associated with the moon.

Although artists throughout the ages have painted them with human faces, they are actually beings of light. Angels can appear to us in many different ways, and usually how we perceive them to be. This could be as a strong white light, a sense of upliftment, as beautiful music or a rainbow of colours, or in their more 'traditional' form with a halo and wings. There is also that saying, "Always be kind to strangers, they could be an angel in disguise!"

Whatever form angels appear to us, we can be sure that they are waiting close by, ready to step forward in our hour of need. And your guardian angel won't mind how you perceive them. The main thing is that you've acknowledged their presence, which helps to open up the bridge between our world and theirs and confirms to them that you believe in their innate power.

They are messengers of the Divine and there are a huge number of celestial beings within the hierarchy of angels. For example, the archangels can help us get the most out of life whether that's through problem-solving, working towards our divine life purpose, goal-setting, seeking financial abundance or loving relationships, or if we need healing.

But they can also help us in more mundane aspects of our daily life such as helping us to find lost objects and guiding us to use our time wisely when working or studying. And I know I'm not the only one to call on the 'parking angels' to help me find a parking space – it works for me every time! However, the angels will not step forward for those who are disrespectful to them or are simply trying to boost their own ego.

As a Reiki Master, I invoke the angels to help me when I carry out any healing and the room can get rather full as I see them stepping forward, all of different sizes and colour but each one assisting with the healing. It really is a sight and a feeling to behold as the room literally buzzes with energy. Sometimes I feel as though I could literally be lifted off the ground! It's a truly euphoric experience. I hope that you, too, will have an angel visitation at some time in your life – there could be one with you right now...

One way to make a closer relationship with the angels is to plan an 'angel day' to show them how much we appreciate their love for us. I have some suggestions here, but everyone has their own unique thoughts and the main thing is that we do whatever feels right and fits in with our home and personal life.

If possible, set aside a whole day for yourself or even with your family all together. Plan it the evening before and write down what you would like to achieve in the company of angels. When you wake up, ask them to bless your day ahead and, in particular, ask your guardian angel to help you to be grounded and aligned, keeping your energy light and bright.

Having a leisurely shower or bath first thing is good as water is cleansing and healing. You may like to add something to the water that reminds you of the angels in some way and helps you relax, perhaps a floral shower gel or an aromatherapy oil that is safe to use in water such as lavender. Enjoy choosing the clothes you will wear too, something light or bright. The angel colours are white, gold, silver, blue, purple, pink, green or lilac. If you especially wish to connect with one of the archangels, then wear blue for Michael, white for Gabriel or green for Raphael. For those who love jewellery, something that contains a crystal such as angelite will add magical energy to your day.

Going for a walk in a beautiful place of nature will help you connect at a higher level with the angels, and you could bring something back home that calls to you such as a feather, a flower, shells or pebbles to paint. These will be a welcome addition to your angel altar if you have one. However, if the weather is too bad to venture outside, you could do something creative indoors such as painting or drawing, writing, even dancing and singing, or just sitting curled up with an angel book. Gardeners could decide to plant something associated with the angels such as honeysuckle, said to attract angels, lilies which represent the Holy Spirit or roses for love and upliftment. In the evening you may like to watch an angel film such as *City of Angels*, *It's A Wonderful Life*, or *Noah*, and relax with a glass of wine.

Inviting the angels into our lives certainly should not be an expensive matter, and it definitely shouldn't be just for Christmas! We don't need to have special skills to be creative and try our hand at making things such as angel jewellery, angel wings, cushion covers, dolls or angel chimes. We can have a go at painting or drawing our own angel pictures, either for the wall or to place on the angel altar.

We can also find lovely items in charity shops such as angel figurines or jewellery and books about angels. Ask your guardian angel to be with you and help you choose the right things for your home. However, remember always to cleanse these things before bringing them into your sacred space. You won't know anything about the previous owner and the energies associated with an object. Do this by saying a blessing or prayer over them, having a lit white candle for purity by your side and, if possible, using a sage smudge stick or white sage incense. Adding herbs such as rosemary and lavender to the mix are also a good idea as they help to protect and cleanse your space. Move the smudge stick or incense gently around in a circular motion, allowing the smoke to completely cover the item to be cleansed.

Things like jewellery and crystals can be washed in cool, fresh water and left to dry in the sunlight. Many crystals can be bought quite cheaply, especially as tumbled stones, and are always a powerful and healing addition to any angelic home. Examples are black tourmaline, selenite, blue kyanite or citrine.

When you are ready, call on your guardian angel to cleanse and bless your items, in your own words or by saying the following prayer.

> *"Dear guardian angel,*
> *Please remove any stagnant energy from this item*
> *and transmute it into love, light and heavenly harmony*
> *as you place a shield of protection around it. Thank you.*
> *So be it."*

As you sit in quiet contemplation, visualise surrounding the item with golden light, then safely blow out the candle and wait until the smoke around your smudge stick or incense has cleared before welcoming your new angel belongings into your home and enjoying placing them wherever feels right to you.

The angels never judge us, they are there to help us and guide us along the right paths in life. But it's always up to us whether we heed their advice or not and, in particular, they will never tell us what to do as we have free will. By universal spiritual laws, they cannot intervene if they are not directed to do so by the Divine. So if we need help we should ask them for a sign, and believe that this will be sent to us at the right time.

Ask, believe and receive.

5
Beliefs about angels

"Angels are not only above us, they are also within us."
(Unknown)

Finding a lovely feather in unusual circumstances can be one of the most beautiful and significant signs from the angels to confirm that they have heard our prayers. It can also be a message from deceased loved ones to let us know, with angelic assistance, that they are at peace in the spirit world. I have come across some special true life accounts showing without doubt that angels can, and will, leave their calling card to comfort us in the most magical of ways.

My own feather story came about when I was staying in hospital with my husband, John, before Christmas one year. He had been blue-lighted there and in the following five weeks was deteriorating before my very eyes. He adored Christmas but was now mentally incapacitated as well as having difficulty in breathing; he had lost a lot of weight and had also lost the use of his legs and was suffering from double vision.

I had so wanted John home for Christmas but the doctor then said that he couldn't leave the hospital after all as he had to have more tests. I was devastated, having arranged for carers to put a hospital bed in at home, and friends having helped me to move the furniture around. I was also worried beyond belief that the doctor was insisting on doing more intrusive tests on a man who was so frail, fearing that he wouldn't survive another lumbar puncture and brain scan.

So, in his hospital room after the doctor had left, I sat and prayed hard to the angels to help make the right decision for John's highest good. After a short while, I felt a shift of energy in the room and then heard John rustling the bed sheets. I opened my eyes, went over to hold his hand, and sitting there on the top sheet was a perfect little white, fluffy feather. I knew in that instance that, not only had the angels heard my prayer, they would know exactly what to do.

My beautiful man passed away just after New Year and three days before he was due to have the tests. A couple of weeks later, my sister and daughter arrived to stay with me, comforting me and supporting me in my grief. The week went by quickly and, on the day they were due to leave for the airport, I knew I wasn't up to going with them to see them off. Our neighbour kindly took them instead.

To keep myself busy, I decided to do a bit of gardening. As I bent down to rake some leaves out of the lavender next to John's motorbike, I saw something white among the leaves. At first I thought it was just a piece of paper but in fact it was the most stunning, large white feather I have ever seen. I tingled from head to foot and silently sent a thank you to John. He was already surpassing himself! If I had gone to the airport with my sister and daughter, I wouldn't have found the feather which convinced me that this was divinely orchestrated.

Shelly tells of a time around nine months after her own partner had passed to spirit when both she and her little daughter had a dreadful sickness bug. Shelly sat on the side of her child's bed crying and crying, at her wits' end, then she shouted out to him, "I just can't do this, I just can't." She then ran into the bathroom to be sick again.

When she came back, her daughter was fast asleep and

looking very peaceful – with a white feather stuck to her cheek. Shelly had no idea how it got there but she took it as a sign from her partner to say, "Yes, you can do it." This strengthened her and their lives soon calmed down. She kept the feather behind a photograph of her and her partner.

Kay also went through a sad and difficult period, receiving chemotherapy for her cancer while at the same time her husband Steve was seriously ill. She had been told there was no hope and it wouldn't be long before it was his time.

"I had one of my chemotherapy sessions a couple of days before Steve passed away, and the next session was after his passing. The nurses asked why I was so upset and I told them that my husband had died a few days earlier. I took out a photograph to show them and one of the nurses even recognised him. As I went to put the photograph away, stuck on my jumper there was a little fluffy white feather. I knew he was with me, giving me strength from above, and it gave me so much comfort."

Gloria asked the angels to send her a clear sign that her Mum was at peace now in the spirit world, having passed recently from a very painful condition. She didn't have long to wait.

"I lived with my Mum and missed her very much. The day after she had passed to spirit I sat down, cried and prayed to the angels. As I came out of the house into the garden, I saw something floating down… it was a beautiful white feather. But that was not all. I felt a beautiful energy around me, urging me to turn around. As I did so I couldn't believe my eyes, there were lots more white feathers settled on the ground in front of the house we shared together.

"I felt really loved and emotional in that moment, seeing all those feathers that seemed to come from nowhere with not a bird in sight. I thanked the angels for giving me the most beautiful sign that my Mum is at peace in the afterlife."

Mafalda tells the story, involving an extraordinary synchronicity, about when she was feeling very lost a few years ago. She asked the angels for divine guidance on whether her true life path was to become a nun or to have a family.

"I asked the question in my meditation class, then within a few moments of starting to walk home I saw a large white feather at my feet. This place was high up on a mountain, not a place where seagulls would hang out and there were no other birds flying around. I took the feather as a sign that the angels had heard my question.

"That evening, I went out to have dinner with my parents. As I was sitting down to eat, a little girl no more than two years-old just ran away from her mother and came to sit on my lap, talking and smiling at me all the time. Her energy was infectious and I knew there and then that she had been drawn to me for a reason and that my answer from the divine was that I would have a family and give birth to a little girl.

"Four years on now and I am happily married. Last year, I gave birth to a beautiful baby girl whom we named Lily. I still have the feather I found and I keep it as a reminder that the angels and the divine are always around us. I still use it to connect with them in my meditations."

Family relationships, however, can often be very difficult yet the angels, full of love and compassion, are always nearby to comfort us. Karen was distraught when her only brother passed away, especially because they had not been close for a while due to family problems with their parents and divorce. One day she was sitting in the bath, talking to him through her tears. Then as she got up to get out of the bath, she saw a small fluffy white feather lying on the bathroom floor.

Heather was separated from her husband but she was still devastated when he became ill and visited him many times when he was in a hospice.

"I was told my husband didn't have long to live. So I asked the angels for a sign that someone he loved would come forward for him when it was his time. A few days later, I was holding his hand in the hospice as he slipped quietly away. The very second he died, a white feather drifted down as if from nowhere. The patio doors were open but there wasn't a breath of wind. The moment felt totally peaceful and comforting, and I knew this was a sign that he was now on his way and free of pain. I thanked the angels for confirming this in such a beautiful way."

Now, not all the feathers that angels will leave for us are white. This is because there may be something specific that the angels want to draw to our attention. So what do the different colours represent?

As we have seen, white feathers are known as 'the calling card' of the angels and will often appear when we have asked for an answer to a prayer. White denotes purity and this is our angel's way of saying, "I have heard your call for help and I am here always."

A blue feather, though, is always associated with communication and is telling us that Archangel Gabriel can help us find an answer to our problem. If there's someone we need to talk to but we're finding it difficult to choose the right words and the right moment, the angels are letting us know that they will help us say the right thing from our heart. On the other hand, a blue feather could also be telling us that we need to listen to others more!

Some people may feel disconcerted when finding a black feather but it's not a bad sign as black absorbs negative energy so it can indicate protection, power and grounding. This could relate to a chapter in our life that is closing, causing us anxiety. Or it may be a sign of our own spiritual awakening, setting out on a new path and putting things into action. A white feather tipped in black means changes are on the way.

The colour green has always represented healing, so a green feather means growth, renewal and healing either for yourself or a loved one. It can also suggest that it would be good to spend more time in nature.

Some other colours are quite rare but they all have their own meanings. Finding a yellow feather is a real blessing. The message being given to us is that we should be happy, contented and grateful, and it's time to focus on what we'd like to manifest in our life. Once we believe that we deserve this, which can be hard for some people, the angels will shower us with abundance.

Purple denotes inner growth. The angels know that we are ready to awaken spiritually, so when we receive a purple feather it's time to sit up and take notice! A brown feather is a gentle reminder that we must ground and align ourselves in order to develop spiritually; it also suggests that we need to be patient and wait for divine guidance. Hopefully, we shall then find a grey feather, telling us that a more peaceful time is forthcoming.

The brighter colours are full of optimism and joy. A red feather represents passion and the need to be aware of our emotions, but it also promises us inner strength. Love and romance are around if we find a pink feather, also a sign of the importance of faith and honour. (It can also predict that there is a baby on the way!) Orange is the colour of creativity so the angels want you to make something wonderful with fresh new ideas.

Finally, a spotted feather is telling us to let go of something or someone that doesn't serve our best interests. It's time to release the pain of the past as we move forward towards new opportunities in the future.

The publisher of this book has his own quirky story about coloured feathers.

"My mother really believed in angel signs, especially feathers. Shortly before she died she said to me, 'Don't worry, I'll send you a white feather to let you know I'm fine.'

"Now, I'm a bit sceptical (or I was then) so I said, 'No, that's too obvious. I want a black feather.'

"A couple of days after she had passed, I went for a walk in some beautiful gardens to clear my mind. I sat on a bench to rest and took out a small book of short stories that a friend had given me recently but I hadn't looked at yet. Opening it at random, I found myself reading a fantasy about a young man who was… covered in black feathers!

"Good one, Mum."

On the theme of feathers, cloud formations in the shape of a feather or an angel can also be a sign in answer to our prayers. A while ago I was at a friend's house and lamenting about certain things that had upset me. I told her that I had asked my guardian angel for help earlier on in the day. I knew she would send a sign that she was helping me but I didn't expect it to come so quickly. Just as I was looking at the beautiful view of the mountains, there above them was a stunning cloud formation in the clear shape of a large angel's wing.

If you have been seeing certain numbers repetitively, the angels are urging you to sit in quiet contemplation as they share further information with you. Perhaps whenever you happen to glance at the clock, for example, you seem to be seeing the same numbers. These may be single numbers, or doubled or trebled numbers, all holding universal energy that can help to guide you along your spiritual path. This is an example of synchronicity, the numbers being in alignment with your thoughts at that particular time, so try to keep your mind as clear and positive as you can.

Here's a strange example of how numbers can be shown repeatedly and what the meaning was behind them, resonating with the important situation in my own life and helping me to move forward in the right way.

When my husband was in a lot of pain, a few days after being sent home from hospital around his birthday, I finally got him settled in bed and waited until he fell asleep before nodding off myself not long after. A few hours later he suddenly awoke, sat up in bed and said, "All the clocks in the house have stopped." The clock in our bedroom showed 2 a.m. as did my phone, and when I checked all our other clocks they also showed 2 a.m. So I went back to bed and told John, saying it must have been a dream.

However, when I woke up the next morning and went into

the living room to make us a cup of tea, I was shocked to see that the clock in that room had stopped at 5.30 a.m. Had John had a premonition? And if so, what did it mean?

I only realised the significance two months later when I got a call from the hospital to say that John had passed away… at 5.30 a.m. Of course, I looked up the angel number 530. It has several meanings but predominantly represents huge life change, protection from the angelic realm and freedom. This gave me some comfort.

Natalie had been seeing the number 11.11 constantly on her clock and wondered what this meant. I explained that this is known as a 'wake-up' sign from the angels who are trying to get her attention; they want her to follow her spiritual path and now was the right time! 11.11 is a 'master number' relating to enlightenment and spiritual awakening.

Natalie agreed that she had been thinking for some time about learning how to meditate as well as how to understand more about the angels and her spirit guide, but kept thinking that she wasn't yet ready. However, the angels disagreed with her! A few weeks later, Natalie started a course and loved every minute of it.

Adele was puzzled because she kept seeing 2.22 or 22.22 everywhere. She said 22.22 has been repeated on her clock and she recently saw 222 as part of the licence plate on the car in front of her when she was driving home. Things came to a head when she opened her book at random to page 222! She had never heard of angel numbers before mentioning all this to me and was immediately intrigued to know more.

Well, seeing 222 repeatedly is a big sign regarding a 'twin flame relationship', perhaps about to come into one's life if single. It is also a sign that things will take a turn for the better in relation to one's career. Adele understood all of this. She was unhappy at work so had applied for a few other jobs; she'd just had an interview for one in particular that went really well. She also said she was ready to find love again in her life. The sequence

BELIEFS ABOUT ANGELS

2222 reinforced the message that she was on the right path in life, so she must trust that all would be well and there would be abundance for her.

Adele contacted me a few weeks later to thank me and fill me in on what was happening. Firstly, the number sequences had now stopped repeating. She was really happy and about to start her new job. Moreover, she would be receiving more money than in her current role, she wouldn't have to travel as far, and she would have flexi-hours which meant a better balance between home and work life. Now she was just waiting for new love to enter her life, trusting that the universe would bring this with divine timing.

If you have been seeing certain numbers repeatedly everywhere, know that your guardian angel is giving you a sign and urging you to look up the meaning. Each single number has its own vibrational meaning as do number sequences or groups. Angel numbers can appear in many ways, like the time on a clock, a car licence plate, being given the same change over and over in a shop or on the shop's till receipt. You may be playing a board game and keep rolling the same number on the die, or a significant phone number calls you just as you're thinking about a certain problem.

All of these experiences are absolutely messages for us to look up the interpretation of the number. There are several helpful websites on the Internet.

Many people say that there are certain numbers that have cropped up regularly throughout their life, and these also hold special meanings for us. For me, it has always been the number 7 and it has always been lucky for me. I used to live at number 7 and we moved house on the 7th. It's even the number I now see every day when I open my window blinds, as it's the number of the house directly opposite mine! The number 7 denotes that the outcome of our dreams will exceed our expectations, and that divine magic is supporting us and opening doors of opportunity.

Another widely held belief is that the angels often send

a rainbow after someone has died. Indeed, perhaps the most famous sighting of a double rainbow is the one that appeared over Buckingham Palace just before the death of Queen Elizabeth II was announced.

The most poignant and emotional rainbow I have ever seen was when I was at the hospital with my husband John a week before New Year, knowing he hadn't got long to live. I have never felt so lost and alone as in that moment, with the thought of never having him in my life again leaving a devastating and dense feeling within my heart.

Many of our friends came to visit him and loved that he had a room with a good view as it overlooked the salt lakes, resplendent with the beautiful pink flamingos that live there. At that time, it didn't bring me any comfort, though, because John couldn't see the view himself being bedridden and too far away from the window. On one particular day he kept pointing to something in the room that only he could see, and I assumed that he could see angels and loved ones who were already here, waiting to guide him over to spirit.

With tears in my eyes, I turned away so he wouldn't see me upset, and looked out of the window. What I saw literally took my breath away, because there it was, a full bright rainbow in the most vivid colours I had ever seen. Within it there was also a lighter rainbow, double arches stretching from one end of the lake to the other.

Now, this was a beautiful sunny day, it hadn't been raining and there was no rain forecast. So I knew it was a sign from the angels that they were with me and John and were surrounding us with love, light and strength for what was to come. A week later my beautiful man stepped out of this life into the next.

Sue shares her rainbow story from when she lived in the Channel Islands. A group of her friends had travelled on a yacht to the Caribbean where, on one of the islands, they'd seen a beautiful cascading waterfall that you could stand near to.

"Our friend Drewy stood in front of the waterfall," she says, "as his wife Vanessa took a photograph. When they looked at it later, it showed a lovely rainbow over him and the waterfall even though they hadn't actually seen a rainbow at the time.

"A year later, Drewy and a few other of our male friends took a boat over to Carteret [on Guernsey] for a visit and to have lunch. Coming back in the dark, they negotiated the steps down a steep hill to reach their boat, moored at the bottom of the stone steps. But Drewy missed his footing, he fell and tragically broke his neck and died instantly.

"His wife Vanessa told me that only the day before the men had gone to Carteret, she had put the waterfall picture on the mantlepiece in a lovely frame. Then, on the day of Drewy's funeral in St. Peter Port, a rainbow appeared over the town."

6
The angelic hierachy

"The angels in all their glory are here to help you to your next step. All you have to do is ask."
(The author)

Because archangels have appeared in many religious texts throughout history, many people believe that they're too remote and we can't ask them for help. Yet I have come to believe that the angels are willing to assist us at any time of night or day, as long as we believe in their presence and have patience as they get to work on our behalf with divine timing.

In my own experience, as well as according to the angel courses I have attended and the relevant research I have done, I have come to believe that the angelic realm is made up of nine groups of angels in Heaven. These are known as ranks, choirs or spheres of angels. Certain ranks are mentioned in the Christian Bible. The Old Testament refers to the Seraphim and Cherubim as well as angels and archangels. In the New Testament, St. Paul mentions the Principalities, Dominions and Powers.

Many believe that the hierarchy of angels in Christianity was developed by Pseudo-Dionysius, a Greek philosopher and theologian whose original name is unknown, and then by St. Thomas Aquinas in the fifth century. They created three choirs of angels, each encompassing three levels, giving us the nine ranks of angels that are written about to this day. Some of the information was gleaned from the Bible and also from the Corpus Areopagiticum, a popular book in Western culture.

On the other hand, it's not only Christianity that taught the hierarchy of angels; there are similar beliefs in Islam and ancient Judaism, which influenced later thinking.

The highest rank of angels are the six-winged Seraphim who reside close to the throne of the Divine; their function is to manage the movement of the heavens. The Cherubim are also very powerful and it is said that they outshine all the other angels. Their function is to attend to God. Images of them look a little frightening, with four wings and four faces of an eagle, a lion, an ox and a human being.

Next we have the Thrones, the third rank within the highest choir, who are believed to be always in the presence of God and (in Christian belief) Jesus. They can be called upon by mankind to help the sick and wounded, and can also be invoked to help heal the universe when it's out of alignment. The Seraphim, Cherubim and Thrones are together known as 'Celestial Councillors'.

The next choir, or group of three, are called the 'Celestial Governors'.

First we have the Dominions whose function is to manage the correspondences of the lower ranks of angels. They are often depicted as holding the seal of God in their left hand and a golden staff in the right. With them are the Powers, the keepers of history and the angels of birth and death. Their role is to protect human beings and, as warrior angels, they are also assigned by the Divine to deal with good and evil within the universe. We can invoke the Powers if we need help to protect our family, home, property and pets.

Finally in this choir there are the Virtues, known as 'the shining ones'. They assist those who are struggling with their faith or the ability to think positively, particularly about themselves.

Once we have asked for their help, the Virtues will send a huge amount of divine energy to help lift us to a place of integrity and worthiness.

The so-called lowest choir of angels are those who are closest to our lives here on Earth. Perhaps lesser known are the Principalities, often depicted as brandishing sceptres and wearing crowns. They have a big job, being the guardian angels of very large groups such as countries, cities and big international organisations. The Principalities are magical angels who can help human beings with the economy, with politics and authorities. They are also said to be the order that assisted David in slaying Goliath.

Most of us know something about the Archangels but they are far from being of 'low rank' because as celestial messengers they can move up and down the hierarchy at the will of the Divine. Each of them possesses their own magical correspondence, the special tasks associated with them, and they love to help us human beings, particularly those who believe in their presence.

Archangels act as a bridge between us and the Divine and can help us with anything we ask of them that genuinely needs divine intervention. For example, we could ask Archangel Gabriel to help us when it's necessary to move house or to find a new job that better suits our talents. We could ask Archangel Metatron for help with healing residual karmic energy from a previous life.

Closest to us are the Angels, also called Guardian Angels, and they are powerful beings in their own right. Each one is assigned to a particular person so our guardian angel will be our angelic companion, friend and confidant throughout our life. Your angel helped you into this world as a baby and, when it's time for you to depart your earthly life, they will guide you over to the afterlife. And throughout our lives, the guardian angels act as a channel between us and the higher ranks of angels.

Although we can call on any of the angels within the celestial hierarchy, the archangels can assist us in our lives on so many levels. It's my belief that they tend to be more accessible than angels in the higher ranks. When invoking the archangels, we can call them by their names.

The word archangel is derived from the Greek word *archi*, which means 'first or principal' and *angelos*, which means 'messenger of God'. They are often described as being 'ruling angels' as they can move up and down the celestial hierarchy at will. As with all angels, they are governed by many universal laws such as human beings having free will. This means they cannot intervene if we go ahead and don't accept their divine guidance, or ignore them entirely!

We should never feel guilty about asking an archangel for help because, as universal spiritual beings, they can respond to anyone's call no matter where or when. For example, if someone in the UK calls upon Archangel Gabriel, and someone else in a different country also calls on her at the same time, she can be there for both people. This is because, like all the higher ranks of angels, archangels are an image of the Divine's omnipresence. They have been named in different religions across the world and throughout history yet they are not aligned with any particular religion; they will hear the call of anyone who asks for their help whether they have religious beliefs or none.

How do I know about the archangels and their work? Well, we never stop learning but I have thoroughly enjoyed attending courses such as Angelic Reiki, Angel Harmonic Healing and Angel Magic, all of which have helped me develop my knowledge. However, the majority of my real connections have come from my own experiences, many of which are included in this book. I have done my own research and there have been many, many personal encounters with angels as well as meeting them in meditation and dreams and during my work.

The more I learn about the archangels, the more I enjoy sharing their magic with others and I have taught many angel workshops over the years. These have included love and relationship guidance with Chamuel, protection, strength and justice with Michael, healing with Raphael, manifestation with Haniel, communication and peace with Gabriel, and wisdom and inner soul magic with Uriel. I feel blessed to be able to connect with the archangels every single day and nothing gives me greater joy than to witness someone who is bursting with joy at being touched by an angel for the first time. They have also helped me in many ways.

The following pages describe information and stories about just those archangels that I have worked with often and extensively over the years. The Warrior Archangel Michael and the Healer Archangel Raphael have been described in other chapters so are not included here.

Archangel Ariel : Protector of the Universe

His name means 'Lion of God' and he is known as the angel of abundance. He is also the angel of nature, with the divine mission to help protect the animals of the world as well as the fairy realm, the 'nature angels'. When we invoke Archangel Ariel to ask for financial gain or abundance in other forms, these often appear when we least expect them.

A mantra to use when we have sought Ariel's help is, "I am manifesting abundant blessings into my life." Keeping the crystal moss agate on our person also focuses our energy.

At a time of financial difficulty some time ago, I was wondering how we would manage as my husband could not work due to illness. And although I was self-employed, mine is not a job where I can guarantee to be working every day. I admit that I was concerned, as anyone would be; yet in my heart I knew we would be okay, I just wasn't sure how.

I asked Archangel Ariel, the angel of abundance, to help us and each time I meditated or drew an angel card I was assured that everything would be fine. This helped me to relax in the knowledge that the angels would take care of things.

A few days later I was working on the manuscript of this book when my phone rang. It was on the 27th at 17.07 and I have already mentioned that 7 is my lucky number. The call was from a company I had contacted a year before regarding an insurance policy that had been sold to us illegally. It had been so long ago that I had forgotten all about it. The caller told me that, indeed, I was being offered compensation, a substantial amount.

When the call ended, I shouted out at the top of my voice, "Wow, thank you, Archangel Ariel!" and I did a happy dance.

Archangel Azrael: The Angel of Grief and Transition

Azrael's name means 'whom God helps' and in literature he is often referred to as the 'angel of death'. But this is far from sinister. Archangel Azrael helps to bring comfort to those who are dying and he greets souls as they pass from the Earth and go towards the light. Importantly, though, Azrael will also comfort those who are grieving. As we go through intense emotions such as shock and stress, and physical symptoms such as depression or panic attacks, he steps forward to absorb the pain we are feeling on all levels.

There are other times, though, when we feel that our lives are going through big and important changes – a transition – and we may feel very anxious, unsure of where we're going. So when we ask Azrael to guide us, a mantra to use is, "I embrace new opportunities in my life." The crystal associated with Archangel Azrael is yellow calcite.

One of the most powerful ways in which we can enlist the help of Azrael is through prayer. First, make sure you are grounded and sitting comfortably in a quiet, comfortable space. When you

THE ANGELIC HIERACHY

feel ready, call Azrael's name three times. After a short while, you may feel a warm energy surrounding you, but don't worry if you can't see or feel him; just by believing and trusting in his heavenly assistance, he will be there.

If this is a time of grief, then you can of course choose your own words in reaching out to Azrael, or you could say the following prayer to help you through the heartbreak.

> *"Dear Archangel Azrael,*
> *Please heal my heart as you wrap your comforting wings*
> *around me in my grief. Please keep my loved one*
> *[say their name here] safe in spirit,*
> *and shower me with the courage and strength I need*
> *as you guide me forward with acceptance in my heart.*
> *Thank you, Archangel Azrael."*

Azrael has often helped me in my spirit rescue work. This can be dangerous and also very emotional, but no more so than when it's a child that hasn't been able to go the light. There was one case that actually occurred in my own home. A medium friend was helping me and we needed celestial help fast!

After being overshadowed by the terrified child spirit a number of times, I eventually 'saw' him walk towards me with water dripping off him, leaving a puddle in his wake. All the while I was relaying what I was experiencing to my spirit rescue partner, and we invoked Archangel Azrael to help set this little boy's soul free. I gasped as I saw warm, open hands reaching out to him, waiting for him to go to them within the light.

After what seemed like an eternity, but was probably ten minutes or so, I heard a noise above us and clearly saw the angel descending as if he had come through the ceiling. His energy was powerful yet gentle at the same time, and he was surrounded by a cream-coloured light. I watched in awe as Azrael took the child's tiny hands in his and wrap him in his mighty wings. The child turned to me and I saw his little face flooded in happiness as they ascended and moved through the bright light until I couldn't see them anymore. At this point I felt such immense peace and knew that the child's soul had flown and he had 'gained his angel wings'.

I drew the Reiki symbols around the room to help cleanse and clear any residual stagnant energy, and went back to the room a little while later. As absolute confirmation that the boy was now at peace with his beloved family, there was a large creamy white feather in the middle of the floor.

Archangel Chamuel : The Angel of Love

Archangel Chamuel is surrounded by a pink ray of light that denotes love, for oneself as well as for others. He will help to strengthen family bonds and pour his love into a heart hardened by negativity. Many of us at times throughout our lives may be scared of opening up our hearts to others, but once this fear is overcome the warmth that Archangel Chamuel brings will be so reassuring, soothing and uplifting.

His name means 'he who seeks God'. We can invoke Archangel Chamuel to improve any existing relationship but he can also help those who feel lonely and want love in their lives. So if you want to find your soulmate, then this is the angel to call on!

A mantra to use is, "I open my heart to love, peace and gratitude." And of course the crystal associated with love and healing is rose quartz.

I had a wonderful experience a while ago as I was working on adding the finishing touches to my 'Archangel Chamuel and the Angels of Love' workshop. My phone beeped and I saw a message on Facebook by Jenny Smedley, a well-known magazine columnist and angel artist. She had posted a portrait of Archangel Chamuel that she had just finished and said she felt that it was "meant for someone". Her friends should let her know if any of them felt it was for them.

Straight away, I had such a strong feeling of an angel's presence around me and I sent her a private message. I asked if she would sell the portrait because I resonate so strongly with Chamuel and was just now even preparing a workshop all about this archangel and love. I also told her about the illness my husband, the love of my life, was suffering and how badly this was affecting me, despite feeling the angelic presence around me when I prayed for help.

Jenny replied saying how sorry she was for what we were going through and promised to send me by email a large copy of Chamuel that would be big enough to transfer onto canvas. I have a friend nearby who specialises in media promotion work and he was able to do just that. It looked amazing and my husband mounted it on the wall behind our bed.

A couple of days later, I woke up and walked into our living room in a sleepy haze and saw the portrait standing up in the corner of the room. I ran back to the bedroom to check and sure enough there was a blank wall, so I asked my husband why he had taken it down.

"I didn't," he said. "When I woke up, there you were fast asleep with the angel picture lying on top of you." He then said that with hindsight he wished he'd taken a photo of it as he'd never seen anything like it before and couldn't believe it hadn't woken me up when it fell on top of me. I was, for want of a better word, gobsmacked! But it also made me tingle and I was sure it was a sign that Archangel Chamuel was protecting us.

My workshop was really enjoyable and successful, and I brought the portrait of Chamuel with me to show everyone. They loved it! So much so, I realised he would be better on the wall in my healing room and there he has had pride of place ever since. He obviously likes it there, too, as he hasn't fallen down.

Archangel Gabriel : The Messenger

Gabriel is often known as the angel of peace and communication and, like Haniel, is also associated with the moon. Personally, I always see this mighty angel as female, despite traditional images.

In mythology, she has also been portrayed with the winged horse Pegasus or a unicorn.

Her name means 'strength of God' and she is often depicted carrying an olive branch, the universal symbol of peace, or a lily flower that represents goddess energy. Therefore, the crystal associated with Archangel Gabriel is moonstone, for femininity, balance and the cycles of life. When we invoke her, we can use the mantra, "I am pure, I am the light."

Naturally, we can call upon Gabriel when there are issues of communication or personal conflict. Interestingly, though, if we are a victim of criminal activity, she will help bring the perpetrator to justice. When Gabriel does step onto our path, she makes things happen quickly, leading to favourable results.

Gabriel is one of my go-to angels. When I had the idea of creating a new set of angel cards, I found myself hesitating and wondering whether I could really make it happen. I reached out to Gabriel who stepped in and pushed me into action. With her divine assistance, the cards were soon hot off the press and so popular they sold out within a couple of weeks. I received wonderful feedback.

Another time, I asked Archangel Gabriel to help me when I had to speak to someone about a delicate matter. The conversation was bound to be difficult. I don't like conflict and had a few sleepless nights about it all, to the point where I must have utterly frustrated Gabriel, if that were possible.

An hour before meeting the person in question, I sat alone in my healing room. I meditated and asked Gabriel and her twin flame, the Lady Hope, to help me choose the right words when speaking. As I sat quietly, I heard a fluttering behind my Reiki treatment bed. Thinking that a butterfly or bird must be stuck there, I went over to take a look: I heard the sound again yet there was nothing there.

Suddenly, I understood – I had heard angel wings, a sign that I was being protected and guided. The meeting went well, I chose the right words from my heart and a big weight was lifted off my shoulders.

Archangel Metatron : The Angel of Ascension

Metatron is thought of as the angel who sits on the throne next to God. He also presides over the Tree of Life and is the angel of empowerment and sacred geometry. There are many images of him surrounded by a three-dimensional cube, the symbol of creation, as it holds the secrets of the universe and helps him to watch over Heaven and Earth.

Metatron has been called the 'angel of life' because it is believed that he takes note of all the good deeds that we human beings do. These are recorded in our personal Book of Life within the Akashic Records, or Halls of Knowledge. This is where the blueprint of every soul who has ever lived on Earth is kept, no matter how many incarnations they have had. We might visualise it as a vast library that stretches out as far as the eyes can see and further.

When reaching out to Metatron, use the mantra, "I am working towards ascension" and the crystal watermelon tourmaline, which helps to provide clarity about the meaning of life.

Archangel Zadkiel : The Holy One

Archangel Zadkiel's name means 'righteousness of God'. He helps us to have mercy and compassion towards ourselves and others, through letting go of judgement and offering forgiveness to those who have hurt us so that we can move forward in our lives. As the angel of mercy, he asks human beings who have done wrong to recognise their mistakes and call on the Divine for help. He helps to transmute negativity into positivity and joy by surrounding us in his violet flame.

When we invoke his assistance he will help us to understand the art of mindfulness as he aids meditation and opens the gateway to our higher mind. Use the mantra, "As I bathe in the violet flame of transmutation, I feel positivity in mind, body and spirit." The crystal associated with Archangel Zadkiel is amethyst, for healing, cleansing our home or helping to refocus an overactive mind.

This story shows that the angels can change our minds, yet in a very natural way. There was a lovely shop not far from where I lived, where I always went to buy things like crystals and incense. I always recommended the shop to my friends and clients, and every time I went there I felt like a child in a sweetshop. The energy was amazing and the owner, Tony, was a lovely gentleman and a mine of information.

One day he advertised a couple of large, absolutely stunning figurines of Archangel Michael and Archangel Metatron. As I already had a couple of smaller Michael figurines, I messaged Tony to say I would like to come and see the other one. He said he would keep it for me but I shouldn't leave it too late as there was only one of each.

A few days later, I went to the shop with my friend Annette, who knew that I was excited to see the Metatron figurine. Tony pointed it out to me and it was indeed beautiful. However, there next to it was a new figurine that had just come in, of Archangel Zadkiel. When I saw this one I was instantly drawn to it and tingled all over, feeling the archangel's presence. This was the one for me.

"Are you sure?" Annette asked. "You said you wanted the other one." I said I was absolutely sure because I had felt the energy around me as soon as I saw Zadkiel. "So do you mind if I buy the Archangel Metatron?"

Bless her, that was the one she had wanted all along but she hadn't wanted to say that as I had gone there for it. So I came out cradling Zadkiel and Annette had Metatron, the angels making us both very happy. My powerful and beautiful Zadkiel figurine now takes centre stage on the angel altar in my healing room.

7
Questions and answers

"When invoked, the angels will help to bring wisdom and understanding from within."
(The author)

The subject of angels is huge and I was guided by my own guardian angel to ask people to send me their questions on social media. I was literally inundated and I have chosen a few of the more difficult or unusual questions to answer here, hoping that you find this useful.

➤ *Are angels and spirit guides one and the same?*

No, they are completely different. Although each of us has one guardian angel and one main spirit guide as our protectors, they differ in that the angels are pure beings of light who have never lived an earthly life and who have never inhabited a human body. They are purely created by the Divine to serve as messengers between the angelic hierarchy and humanity.

For example, our guardian angels are those we are closest to as they have been assigned to us personally and they hear our every thought and every prayer. Then there are the archangels whom we can also invoke, as these powerful beings possess their own magical correspondences so we know which one to communicate with for whatever particular help we need.

Just like our guardian angels, though, everyone also has a spirit guide who has been assigned to us individually. Yet our spirit guides have lived in a human body. They are ascended spirits from the human line of evolution and therefore have had spiritual experiences themselves similar to those we encounter in our own lifetime.

Our spirit guides are there to help guide us along our spiritual path in life; and who better to guide us than someone who understands what it is like to have lived on Earth? Now ascended beings, our spirit guides are pure spirit and have no ego.

Our main guide is often known as our 'doorkeeper' or 'gatekeeper', and they are the one who is assigned to us before we are born to help guide us in understanding life's many lessons. These lessons could be experiences that have not been resolved from a previous life, so we have been given the chance to be reborn and find a solution to those problems in this lifetime (referred to as 'past life karma'). Our main spirit guide will stay with us throughout our entire lives and help us to fulfil our earthly missions.

Other guides may make themselves known to us at different intervals on our paths. How we meet our spirit guide is a personal experience and is unique to each of us, be it through meditation or another form of spiritual development.

> *Why do guardian angels allow bad things to happen to us?*

The angels are celestial beings of light and as such are close to the Divine who gave mankind free will. Unfortunately, all through history mankind has violated this freedom. Because of this, evil occurs as well as goodness. So the reason our guardian angels cannot stop awful things happening to us is because they cannot meddle with someone's free will.

However, it is my belief that although they cannot stop certain difficult things happening to us, they often step in to ensure the outcome isn't as bad as it might have been.

➤ *Is there a specific time or day to call on the angels?*

Many people ask me when it's best to call on the angels for help. From the work I have done over the years, I have found that we can call on them at any time, day or night, and on any day of the week. However, I find it's best when there is less interference such as phones ringing, having the television on, people talking and distractions such as busy street traffic.

➤ *Do all faiths have the same beliefs about angels?*

Although different faiths may call the angels by other names, they are always seen as beings of light and divine protectors. For example, in Christianity the archangels are seen as messengers or servants of the Divine, with different ranks within the angelic hierarchy.

Zoroastrianism was named after a Persian prophet, Zarathushtra, as described in Chapter 1. It is recorded in the holy text *Gathas* that an angel appeared before Zarathushtra and introduced him to Ahura Mazda, an ancient god known as 'the supreme creator', who spoke to Zarathushtra about the order of angels via visions and dreams. Zoroastrianism was originally recognised as a religion during the Persian empire, around 550 to 330 BCE.

According to this faith, Ahura Mazda is the God who created the world: the Earth, mankind and the hierarchy of angels as messengers.

In ancient Judaism, leading to the modern Jewish faith, angels are spiritual beings yet can appear in human or other forms. They are seen as messengers and the servants of God, with no free will of their own, and collectively known as Malakim – a reminder to the people that God is within and around us all the time. They make up the sixth of ten ranks of angels, defined in the writings of the Sephardic rabbi Moses ben Maimon, commonly known as Maimonides, who lived from 1138 to 1204 CE. These ten ranks differ considerably from the nine ranks described earlier in this book. Other Judaic writings, though, do refer to the archangels Michael, Gabriel and Raphael.

Muslims believe that the angels were created as light beings by their god, Allah, and that each angel has been assigned their own specific function. For example, there are angels who oversee health, wealth, even the weather, as well as those who record a person's deeds during their lifetime. It is said that one angel sits on the right shoulder to record all good deeds and another sits on the left shoulder to record all bad deeds! In Islam it is believed that the Qur'an was given by Allah to the prophet Muhammad by the Archangel Gabriel.

Buddhists have a rather different view of angelic beings. Devas are light beings with individual personalities and paths in life. They are not immortal or omniscient, and they rarely get involved in human life. Other celestial beings are Tennin, originally feminine spirits of the clouds and waters who figure prominently in Asian arts, and Niō, the fierce guardians of the Buddha.

There are many different offshoots of Buddhism but generally the celestial beings are thought of as protective. They also help to bring peace and purity to the minds of people who follow 'the Five Precepts' that describe how to live an ethical life.

In Hinduism, angels are called devas, or suras, meaning 'shining ones' or 'heavenly beings'. Deva is the masculine form and devi the feminine. The oldest Vedic texts speak of thirty-three devas, eleven each for the three worlds of Heaven, Earth and mid-air. Each deva has special responsibility and magical powers, called siddhis.

Hinduism is not monotheistic and all the devas are worshipped equally as 'supreme beings'. In particular, Brahma, Vishnu and Shiva, form 'the Trimurti' whose task is to ensure that the cosmos functions correctly and that evolution develops well.

People of the Hindu faith also worship guardian angels, who are different to those of other religions. They help people to form closer relationships and can indeed appear in human form, seen as beautiful or handsome people.

The Mormon church, part of the Latter Day Saint religion, was founded by Joseph Smith in the New York of the 1820s who said that God and Jesus both appeared to him in a vision to tell him that existing Christian denominations were "all wrong". Mormons believe that all people have godliness within them, and that angels (who do not have wings) are spirit children of God who are sent to deliver His messages, teach people true beliefs, save them from danger and guide them in doing God's work.

➤ *How can archangels be in more than one place at a time?*

Celestial beings are not restricted by time and space like we humans are, so they can answer the call of more than one person no matter where they are geographically. This is because the angels can respond at the speed of thought.

➤ *How can the angels help me manifest my desires?*

The most positive way of manifesting our desires is by saying positive affirmations. We could start by saying something short and sweet such as, "I love and believe in myself." This should make us feel good.

Angel affirmations are positive and all-powerful statements we can say to help us move forward in our lives as we start to manifest our desires. One way to explain affirmations is that when we think of something positive, in a word or a sentence for example, it can make us feel happy even to the point of smiling and lighting up our face. Well, affirmations are taking things one step further as they are made up of positive thoughts, words and happy vibes, which help to rewire our brains, inspiring us and boosting our confidence, filling our minds with positive endorphins. And as if that isn't enough, they can also help to raise our self-esteem.

Affirmations such as "I AM" are all-powerful, especially if said in the right way and out loud. Saying affirmations out loud strengthens the link between us and the angelic realm as it raises the energy and promotes positivity on all levels. The angels love to hear our voices!

Some people say they have used affirmations in the past and felt that nothing has happened, becoming dispirited at the first hurdle. But as soon as we start to feel that nothing is happening, this is exactly what will be reciprocated because negative thoughts are also energy-based. The most wonderful things in life do manifest when we are patient and believe in divine timing: what we wish for comes to us at the right time.

The key is to say our affirmations out loud and to believe and trust in the process. The auditory sound of our voices also works with our subconscious minds; thoughts and words are powerful, creating energy in one way or another, so keep them positive.

If you feel that you can't say your affirmations out loud for any reason, then there is nothing wrong with saying them silently to yourself as long as you have patience in the outcome and trust that they will manifest in time. Many people say they can't say affirmations out loud because they live with others who do not share the same beliefs. Well, the solution is to have a space of your own within the house where you are not going to be disturbed, and say your affirmations daily with ultimate belief in your heart. An alternative, of course, is to go into the garden if you have one, or go for a walk, especially in a beautiful place of nature.

Naturally, we should also be conscious of how we say our affirmations. If we say them as though we don't really believe in them, then they are not going to manifest. If we are saying them in a bored way, they will not be reciprocated.

The best time for affirmations are after grounding and aligning in the mornings. Then, if there is an opportunity later in the day, we can repeat them. Some like to say theirs out loud while doing the housework, which may even help us to finish the work earlier!

Everyone can choose their own words for angel affirmations but here are a few to get started with, some of my own as well as those of others who sent me their favourites on social media.

> *"I am blessed to be working with the angels*
> *who guide me to my next step.*
> *I am healthy in mind, body and spirit.*
> *I am ready to manifest my dreams.*
> *I am strong and courageous like the phoenix rising from the fire.*
> *I am ready to embrace positive change in my life,*
> *I believe in myself and I can achieve anything I put my mind to.*
> *I give thanks to my guardian angel who guides me along the right path in life."*

Joseph tells me that he has used the following affirmation for years and it has helped him through challenging times.

> *"My personal self, my living space and my heart*
> *will only be filled with light, love, harmony,*
> *peace, joy, balance, wisdom and abundance."*

Atalia says that a few months ago she was sitting in her garden in the sun and thought about all the times she felt 'dressed' by the attitudes of others and their toxic energy. All of a sudden, she realised that from now on she was going to 'dress herself'. So whenever she feels a bit uncomfortable, negative or in low spirits, she says the following affirmation:

> *"Let's go and dress your day. How do we want to dress it?"*

Paul rides a motorbike and knows how dangerous that can be. So before he goes out for a ride he says:

> *"I thank my angels and ancestors for keeping me safe on the road today and every day."*

Elizabeth's favourite affirmation is:

> *"I am a beautiful and wise warrior woman, ready to walk towards healthy and happy times."*

It's always important that our intentions are clear.

> *"Dear angels, my ultimate goal is to [.......] in my life. Thank you for opening new doors of opportunity before me by sending in the right people, positive thoughts, and signs and omens that will manifest my dreams into reality. And so it is, thank you."*

➤ *How do I know whether information in books about the angels is the truth? Some of it seems generalised and some books have conflicting information.*

No two authors are the same. Some may write about what they have experienced personally, whereas others may only repeat information they have researched. Yes, it can be difficult to differentiate between what has been generalised and what is fact.

Moreover, each person may be reading a certain book with a different attitude or for a different reason. Perhaps one reader wants information about true angel visitations, and another about how to connect with their guardian angel. Even if we read about the same subject in two different books, they will be written in different ways as each author will have their own beliefs and experiences, not to mention their own writing skills.

We have to decide which authors to trust, based on how their information resonates in our hearts.

QUESTIONS AND ANSWERS

➤ *What is the meaning of an archangel's twin flame?*

It is believed by many that the archangels each have a feminine complement known as their 'twin flame' who helps the angel make up 'the seven rays of light', often associated with the seven colours of the rainbow. These rays represent the ways in which each coupling can assist mankind through their divine love and healing, guided by the Divine. The twin flames are often referred to as 'Archeia'.

Personally, I prefer to call them purely by their names because, although they are powerful ascended beings, I don't believe they are angels since they have lived an earthly life before ascending to a higher vibration within the universe.

1st ray: Archangel Michael and the Lady Faith. The colour of this ray is blue and it represents faith, protection, power, courage and strength.

2nd ray: Archangel Jophiel and the Lady Christine. Their yellow ray represents wisdom and illumination.

3rd ray: Archangel Chamuel and the Lady Charity make up the third ray of light in the colour pink, bringing divine love and peace.

4th ray: Archangel Gabriel and the Lady Hope bring a ray of white light, the colour of purity, divinity and peace.

5th ray: Archangel Raphael and the Mother Mary make up the fifth ray of light in the colour green for divine healing.

6th ray: Archangel Uriel and the Lady Aurora. Their ray is red, which stands for wisdom.

7th ray: Archangel Zadkiel and the Lady Amethyst bring a ray of light in the colour purple, denoting mercy and transformation.

> *I have heard the term 'Elohim' several times but am not sure what it means.*

This word means 'mighty one' or 'supreme being', and is the Hebrew term for God as the creator of the universe. But the word has at times been used to refer to anyone who is powerful and is held in the highest esteem, such as rulers or judges.

> *Do angels really leave feathers when they are nearby? And if I don't receive any, does this mean my angel is not with me?*

Your angel will always be around you and they do often leave feathers when they are nearby. A white feather is known as the angels' 'calling card' and they will be found in unusual places where you know there are no birds around. I find that feathers appear when I am not looking or am least expecting them.

Ask your guardian angel to leave you a sign and believe with all of your heart that they will. Trust is the key here and there is no need to keep making the same request as this shows doubt and can block the process. Just be ever-present and know that your feather will be presented to you with divine timing.

However, feathers are only one sign that the angels can send as confirmation they have heard our prayers. There could be a significant cloud formation, a butterfly or robin, or repetitive number sequences on a clock or even on car number plates. Our intuition will let us know if this is indeed a sign from our angel. There is more about this in Chapter Five.

> *How is an angel chosen to be the guardian for a new life to begin on Earth?*

It is my belief that only the Divine will know which angels are to be assigned to new human lives. But it's something that none of us will understand fully in this lifetime as we are on a much lower vibration than the angelic world of light. All we can do is trust that all is as it should be, and that each angel has been chosen to guide a particular human being for the right reasons.

> *What is a fallen angel?*

It is believed that a fallen angel is one who has turned away from the divine path and as a result has been banished from Heaven. Mythology tells the story of Lucifer, once a powerful angel loyally serving God. But greed and self-interest got the better of him and he wanted divine power for himself, so he created his own army of angels to help him defy God.

But Archangel Michael and his legion of loyal angels was far stronger and Lucifer, also known as Satan or the Devil, was cast down to Earth along with other rebel angels. According to the Book of Enoch, there were two hundred of them. These fallen angels are often described as demons, malevolent beings who roam the Earth in order to cause harm to mankind, for example by influencing individuals to take drugs, become alcoholics or get involved in crime.

> *Are the little baby angels we often see in paintings the Cherubim mentioned in the Bible?*

No, they are completely different. The Cherubim, along with the Seraphim, are the highest rank of angels within the celestial hierarchy and as such are extremely powerful. The chubby 'babies with wings' that you are referring to are called 'cherubs', yet they have never been mentioned in the Bible or other religious texts.

One of the most famous paintings of cherubs is *Madonna and Child with Cherubs*. It was painted by the artist Rosso Fiontino between 1512 and 1517 CE. Since then, particularly around Valentine's Day, a cherub has often been shown with bow and arrows and called Cupid, representing the birth of a loving relationship.

➤ *Why do people criticise others for believing in the angels?*

Sadly, many people think they know 'the truth' and criticise others who disagree with them. So it may just be because they don't believe that angels exist or because their own religion has different dogma. Sometimes, too, it's as simple as a fear of the unknown.

➤ *Who are the angels of the forest?*

This is a term to describe the fairy realm. Although they are not angels as such, people believe they are like them because they have wings and can fly. They are known to be spiritual beings that live in woodland areas, forests and parks, or by water. They have been written about for centuries in many cultures around the world and are celebrated to this day during the festivals of the seasons which make up 'the Wheel of the Year'. If you have ever seen silvery sparkles, you may have been in the company of a fairy or two!

➤ *Is it true that there are angels linked to the zodiac signs?*

In recent times, many have come to believe that the four main archangels are associated with the astrological signs.

Michael assists those born under the signs of Aries, Leo and Sagittarius.

Raphael is the angel who helps those born under the signs of Gemini, Libra and Aquarius.

Gabriel is associated with those born under the signs of Cancer, Scorpio and Pisces.

Uriel assists those born under the signs of Taurus, Virgo and Capricorn.

➤ *Can an archangel be my guardian angel or spirit guide?*

I don't believe that they can be either. Archangels are powerful beings that are assigned their duties by the Divine and have a higher vibration than the angels assigned to us at birth, our guardian angels. Nor can they be spirit guides as they are pure beings of light.

By contrast, our spirit guides have lived on the Earth, performing good deeds throughout each incarnation and becoming what is often described as 'ascended beings'. It is at this level that they are assigned to particular human beings as their spirit guides in order to help them along their paths in life.

8
The healing ambience

"Angels are inseparable friends who bring strength and consolation to those who include them in their lives."
(Gustave Flaubert)

A lady came to see me, utterly distressed and feeling that the angels had deserted her. Let's call her Verity. She was in such an emotional state as she had lost two babies through miscarriage and was scared to get pregnant again in case the same thing happened, although she wanted to have a child more than anything in the world. She had been praying to the angels, asking them to help her get pregnant and give birth to a healthy baby.

A friend had suggested that she might have an Angelic Reiki treatment, as Verity had told her she was "all over the place". She hadn't heard of it before so she did a little research for practitioners in the local area and my name kept popping up. It was a while before she made contact as at first she didn't think her prayers to the angels had been heard. But it got to a point when she said she couldn't ignore the synchronistic ways in which she kept seeing or hearing my name in different scenarios. A friend of hers had had a psychic reading with me, for example, and another friend lent her a copy of my first book. Verity booked her Angelic Reiki session with me.

During her treatment she relaxed straight away and, as I called for the angels to carry out the treatment, I felt a rush of energy in the room as if a lot of people had entered although at that moment I couldn't see anything. I didn't have to wait long. All of a sudden I felt my hands vibrating over her solar plexus where I saw stunning blue lights and I felt a hand over mine guiding me. I just knew it was the protective energy of Archangel Michael.

The next thing I felt, as I moved my hands over her heart, was what I can only describe as an invisible group hug around both of us. When I looked down, I saw green and white twinkling lights moving around the area and I sent a silent thank you to Archangel Raphael, the angel of healing.

Then I had the most wonderful vision, an image of an angel holding a beautiful baby dressed head to toe in blue. I just knew that the angels were telling me that Verity would eventually give birth to a healthy baby boy. Sure enough, a few months later she called me to say she was pregnant again; she eventually gave birth to her first baby, a healthy boy. She and her husband named him Michael after, yes, the archangel.

Annette is a spiritual medium in the UK and she shared her story with me. She had been to a local Spiritualist centre where the medium gave her a message from her Mum, who was quite insistent that she should go for a blood test. Annette was puzzled by the message as she hadn't felt unwell.

However, a few days later she learned that her son's partner, Lucy, who had suffered two miscarriages early in pregnancy, had to go to her doctor for a check-up. He asked her for a urine sample which she couldn't do, so he sent her for a blood test instead. The results showed that she was suffering from a rare form of leukaemia, which would not have been detected if she hadn't had the blood test. Lucy was soon admitted to hospital to start her treatment.

This was an example of a spiritual message that might not have been passed on perfectly correctly, yet proved that our loved ones in the afterlife, guided by the angels, are still with us and caring for us.

Well, there was more to come. During one of Annette's meditations she saw an image of Albert Einstein who showed her a blackboard with E=mc² written three times. She was puzzled, of course, so asked what it meant and he replied, "Just use your technology" – in other words, search the Internet! When she searched for the spiritual meaning of the equation, the result was 'the Christ consciousness'. So it seemed that powerful angelic forces were at work...

Later, she saw another vision of Lucy in hospital, with Einstein and a few doctors standing around her bed. Einstein was holding a large syringe at Lucy's left arm. Annette asked what he was doing and he told her not to worry, to trust him, as he was "taking something out and putting something in". This would "eradicate pharmaceutical companies" because Lucy would become part of clinical trials with a new, progressive consultant. He also predicted that she would baffle the medical profession and would have a child naturally.

Annette visited Lucy in hospital later and told her about her meditations and what Einstein had said. She confirmed that, yes, she was now part of a special clinical trial and had a wonderful new consultant and cancer nurse. A few days later, her partner Jake reported that the doctors were baffled, as Lucy was out of bed walking properly and her immune levels were now normal. A short while later, she rang the bell of recovery.

The following year, Lucy asked at her regular check-up appointment whether she would be able to get pregnant after all, now that her immune levels were normal, but was told that she would need IVF due to the cancer treatment. She should also allow her body to recover for at least a year. Within a few months, however, Annette received a call from Jake to tell her that Lucy was pregnant. It was a difficult pregnancy with a rare placenta, but again she baffled the consultant looking after her who had never known a woman conceive naturally after such a serious illness.

Lucy gave birth to a healthy boy, Charlie, at thirty-four weeks and he has grown up perfectly normally. Annette says that even at four years-old he was constantly asking her questions about angels and the spirit world!

Jane told me about her experience when she attended one of my angel workshops. At one point, I had invoked the highest angelic healers and their twin flames and then led the group in a meditation with Archangel Raphael and his twin flame, the Lady Mary. I told the group to speak to Raphael, the healer, and tell him of any pain they were suffering, asking for his help.

During the meditation, Jane said, she felt his green ray of light around her so asked for his help with her right eye. Recently, something like a piece of skin at the back of the eye that looked like cellophane was flicking across and obscuring her central vision. This was dangerous, especially when driving at night as she couldn't see properly.

Jane was aware of the presence of Lady Mary accompanying Archangel Raphael, holding Jane's head and stretching it upwards so much that she felt, in her own words, like a giraffe! The next day, Jane turned the television on for the news and realised that she could read the small text scrolling at the bottom of the screen clearly. Whatever had been hindering her eyesight had just gone.

Corinna is a Reiki Master and she told me two stories of incredible angelic help. One lady was suffering with uterine cancer and came for Reiki treatments.

"In the healing sessions she had with me, there were always three angels that came in to assist. They wore white clothes to cleanse her energy and they felt very gentle, floating into the room within white light. I had never seen that before in previous sessions. They would lovingly wipe down her body inside and out with sparkling white cloths made of light.

"When the lady went for surgery later, the surgeon was surprised to find that the cancer was gone. And after all her follow-up appointments the cancer never returned and she did not need radiation treatment."

Another of Corinna's clients was in a car accident and was

stuck inside the vehicle. A man showed up and helped her escape the vehicle, then stayed by her side until the paramedics arrived. He even watched over her as they put her in the ambulance. The next day she reached out to the paramedics to see if they had a name of the person who had helped her, so she could thank them. They said that when they arrived there was no-one else there other than her.

"She came to me," said Corinna, "to get confirmation of who that was. As she was asking the question, I could see an angel appear behind her. He appeared as a man in his late thirties, thin with brown hair, and I described how he was dressed. She started to cry as this was exactly the figure she had seen. She really had been saved by an angel."

During a routine gynaecological check-up, the doctor found a cyst on Mari's left ovary. He said they may have to intervene surgically as it was quite large.

"A few nights later," Mari says, "I was doing a yoga workout as I find that moving my body in that way helps me to connect to the Divine more easily. During a particular pose, I went into a meditation and asked my guardian angel for clarity on the cyst issue.

"Immediately, I felt myself surrounded on all four corners by angels, and Archangel Michael was supporting my head. In my mind I was shown all the instances in this lifetime and the past where my identity as a woman had been abused and belittled. Throughout this witnessing process, I felt Archangel Michael's loving support. There were tears as I watched the events unfold, stories I wasn't even consciously aware of.

"All the while I felt surrounded and supported by the angels, to the point where my whole body was vibrating by the time I finished. A few days later, I went back to the doctor for another scan and the cyst was completely gone."

The angels are divine healers and can be invoked at any time to help heal something in our lives. If, like many other people, you are struggling with health issues whether physical, emotional, psychological or spiritual, know that you can call on the angels to guide you to take the right step towards a balanced and healthy life.

Sometimes when we ask them for healing they will help in a gentle way, such as in a dream or with a thought that leads us to the healing method we need. At other times it can be powerful or dramatic, as we have seen in the stories above. When we ask the angels in general to help or speak to a specific angel such as Archangel Raphael, the healing has started already as we have taken a step in the right direction by believing in their heavenly assistance.

Have you ever visited somewhere in the world that left you feeling full of love, energised and uplifted, without knowing why? This is all about energy. We cannot see it but it is there, and it's not always about seeing the beauty of a place, it's how it makes us feel. So if we need to leave behind all the stresses of everyday life, to receive angelic healing and cleanse our minds, attending an angelic retreat could be a very uplifting experience.

Nowadays, there are quite a few angelic retreats advertised. But please don't assume that the more expensive a place is, the better it is. That isn't necessarily true at all. The angels always want what is best for you, so if you do decide to go ahead and book a retreat, rather than getting bogged down with the plethora of information online, sit and meditate for a while. Ask your guardian angel to guide you to the place that is right for you. With divine timing, that information will come to you either through a meditation, a thought, or some synchronicity that keeps recurring.

You may like to keep an angel journal, a wonderful way in which to make notes and write down dreams or meditations; or you could actually write a letter to your angel asking them to guide you to the perfect place, where you will meet like-minded souls and enjoy some much needed rest and rejuvenation with your guardian angel by your side.

A while ago I myself wanted to attend an angel retreat. However, I couldn't find anywhere within my price range. So I spoke to my guardian angel who suggested that I should teach an angel retreat myself... Now, why didn't I think of that in the first place?

I felt excited by the idea, especially when a friend said that I could hold the event at her home. I knew this would be perfect as she lives in a large villa with its own pool and lots of open space. So I set about writing down my ideas for the retreat in my angel journal and came up with the magical content, which I discussed and agreed with my friend.

As soon as I advertised it, a very reasonably priced one-day angel retreat, it was booked up within a few days. Included in the price was a healthy lunch, a relaxing swim in the pool, angel meditations, healing by Archangel Raphael and an angel reading with me. We had a wonderful day when we could all feel the angels around us, for they rejoice when we are having fun. So you see, you don't have to pay a fortune to enjoy a beautiful, relaxing day for yourself with like-minded people and surrounded by the love and light of the angels.

My guardian angel also guided me to share a little information about something rather different. Etheric retreats are places that hold the magic of healing energy yet cannot be seen with the human eye as they vibrate at such a high rate. Each of these stunning areas has been created by the Divine in order to help mankind and is guarded by specific archangels and their corresponding twin flames, as well as by ascended masters. Such a retreat is called a 'temple of light' where every form of healing takes place, from saving souls who lost their lives by suicide or those who are not yet ready to go to the next life. During this time of out-of-body or near-death experience, they receive intense healing. Many believe that human souls may reside here for rest periods between each incarnation, and newly ascended beings are trained here in readiness for their divine life missions.

Although we cannot enter these places in physical form, it's believed possible for living human beings to visit an etheric retreat during sleep, through meditation or by attunement to specific healing modalities. During meditation in one of my angel workshops, we entered one of the etheric retreats and everyone had a profound and uplifting experience as they journeyed within. You don't have to see to believe.

There are many physical, very spiritual sanctuaries across the world, some of which have a reputation for healing people on all levels. I shall just mention two of them here because of their miraculous and historical connection.

Lourdes in France is one of the most famous healing places in the world. The story is that, in 1858, the Virgin Mary appeared eighteen times to a fourteen year-old peasant girl called Bernadette Soubirous. The girl was told to dig into the ground at a certain spot and when she did so a spring appeared, now called the Grotto of Massabielle. Bernadette was told that this spring water had healing qualities and before long stories of miraculous healing were spreading far and wide. Nowadays, many millions of people make a pilgrimage to visit the blessed grotto of Lourdes for healing.

The Virgin Mary also appeared before three shepherd children near Fátima, in Portugal, six times between 13th May and 13th October, 1917. They saw her surrounded by a bright light and she spoke to them, saying that she was the Lady of the Rosary and making prophesies about the future. Finally, she told the children that God would perform a miracle on 13th October, their final vision, so that people would believe what she prophesised would happen.

On that date a crowd of around fifty thousand people gathered and, it is said, the little shepherd boy Lucia shouted, "Look at the sun!" As everyone looked up to the sky, dark clouds parted as if by invisible hands and the sun appeared silver, spinning around the clouds. People cried, screamed and fell to their knees in awe, surrounded by a stunning blue light that eventually turned to yellow. Some people later said they had seen the face of the Blessed Virgin in the sun, whereas others described that it was spinning so fast as it started to shake they thought it was going to fall out of the sky.

The Sanctuary of Our Lady of the Rosary of Fátima, where 'the miracle of the sun' occurred, is also now a place of healing pilgrimage visited by up to five million people each year.

There are many angelic healing sanctuaries, modalities and organisations throughout the world. One approach that is very dear to me is Angelic Reiki. Since being trained as an Angelic Reiki practitioner, and then becoming an Angelic Reiki Master Teacher, it has seemed as though my whole world has come alive and I feel so much closer to the angelic worlds.

The official international website of Angelic Reiki tells the story of how it was created. The course was written by Kevin and Christine Core in 2002, after seven years of intense work channelling the guidance of mighty Archangel Metatron and the Tibetan monk and ascended master Djwal Khul. From these ancient teachings has come a worldwide accredited healing course which, I can honestly say, is one of the most beautiful and profound healing modalities I have ever experienced.

This new healing approach combines ancient wisdom with an updated perspective that suits the modern world, and is something pure, empowering and uplifting. It is the angels who are the healers in this modality. Angelic Reiki's core belief is that the angels help to release imbalances in the body that are then brought into alignment as emotional trauma is released, creating a positive flow of energy throughout the body and mind. This comes about 'by divine teamwork' as, during an angelic healing session, the practitioner acts as a bridge to bring forward the perfect angels to help heal the client.

Archangel Metatron is a powerful angel, referred to as 'the

angel of empowerment' because his name means 'to guide' and he assists human beings to stop procrastinating and, instead, move forward on our spiritual paths in life. As described before, he is also known as the keeper of all human deeds, past, present and future, recorded in our personal 'books of life'.

The monk Djwal Khul taught the esoteric tradition of the Ageless Wisdom, the principles of the world's great philosophies that help the spiritual evolution of the Earth. These teachings were channelled through Alice A Bailey, who wrote twenty-four books between 1919 and 1949. They are published by the Lucis Trust.

After Kevin Core passed away, Christine took over the helm of Angelic Reiki and is still a professional healer, teacher and conference presenter.

There are many spiritual healers in the world today, people who have a natural gift of healing by channelling universal energy to help others in mind, body and soul. Spiritual healing is holistic and not related to any religious practice. In recent generations there have been some quite exceptional healing individuals.

For example, Edgar Cayce (1877 – 1945) was an American healer and clairvoyant who became known as 'the Sleeping Prophet' as he would slip into a trance state when he shared spiritual information, such as about reincarnation and the Great White Brotherhood, as well as make predictions of world events. Especially important, though, was his ability to diagnose clients' illnesses, receiving psychic information during trance. Then he might prescribe certain remedies or actually give healing himself.

In 1925 the Cayce Hospital was opened so that he could give medical care to his patients, based on his trance readings. The information was given by the spiritual world and Cayce's philosophy was, "The spirit is the life. The mind is the builder. The physical is the result."

Harry James Edwards was born in 1893 in Islington, London. After an early career in printing, service in World War I and failed political ambitions, he happened to attend a Spiritualist church in 1935 to watch the mediums giving their demonstrations. One of the mediums there told Harry that he had the gift of healing, which he soon put into practice with some spectacular results. In a short time, his success in helping people who were in immense pain and suffering to get back on their feet again was being passed on by word of mouth.

He became so much in demand that he had to abandon his home and move with his family to a far bigger house with surrounding land, at Burrows Lea in Surrey. Here he set up his healing practice, the Harry Edwards Healing Sanctuary. He never charged money for his work, only accepting voluntary contributions.

Edwards was a spiritual healer, a teacher and an author who dedicated his life to his unique gift for over thirty years. Known as a man of great humility and compassion, he gave healing to people in person as well as giving many mass public demonstrations of his ability. Through distant healing, he became known throughout the world and even during World War II he served in the Home Guard and practised healing for those who had been injured in the war.

The National Federation of Spiritual Healers (NFSH) was founded in 1954 to help promote healing and to teach professional and honourable standards in all healing practices. Edwards helped to develop this work and became the Federation's first President, designing a training programme for healers that has led to many working in around sixteen hundred hospitals in the UK.

He passed away in 1976 but his legacy still lives on at the Sanctuary, where healers he had trained continue the work of spiritual healing for people as well as for animals.

More recently, one of the most extraordinary healers was George Chapman (1921 – 2006), an English trance medium and healer from Bootle, England, who practised for over sixty years. In his mid-twenties, during an informal meeting with friends, he was more than a little surprised when they told him he'd slipped into a trance and channelled a deceased ophthalmic surgeon from Middlesex Hospital, William Lang, who had passed away a decade earlier. Later meetings with Lang's daughter and granddaughter confirmed that all the detailed information the surgeon gave was accurate.

Lang insisted that Chapman was a medium with healing ability and said that he would work through him. So began an incredible partnership between the two, with diagnoses of illnesses and many psychic operations being successfully performed. During these sessions, George's mannerisms and even his appearance took on the persona of an older man, speaking in an educated voice with a different accent. These were perfectly characteristic of Lang, according to family and friends.

During their collaboration, they brought about healing to thousands of people. The medium would lay his hands on the patient and Lang would 'operate' on them, often calling on other spirit doctors to help including, later, his own deceased son, Basil. Miraculous healing was given to people suffering from brain tumours, cataracts, retinal detachments, breast cancer, leukaemia, hepatitis and many other conditions.

In 1958, George Chapman founded the Birmingham Healing Centre to provide medical assistance locally due to the high demand in that city. Then, in his later years, George referred patients to his son, Michael, who has continued spiritual healing, supported by Basil's spirit.

There are, of course, many thousands of spiritual healers – and those working with other alternative methods – the great majority of whom will never be well-known. But it is inspiring to know that those in the spiritual worlds are close, willing and able to help us.

9
Elements and earth angels

"Set your life on fire, seek those who fan your flames."
(Rumi)

I learned about the elemental angels during my studies and research, and have since called on them to assist in many different ways. Air, fire, water and earth are the elements at the heart of the material world and without even one of them our planet would not exist.

In ancient times, the four elements were considered the building blocks of the universe and spiritual leaders studying nature and the stars wanted to understand how God created the Earth and how they could connect with the elements in order to develop the lives of their people. Even in our modern day, we all live and breathe the elements with every breath we take, as we warm ourselves beside the fire, wash ourselves in water and walk upon the land. It is something we take for granted yet without these elements we would not survive. Each of the elements represents an emotion in order to focus our minds.

Air stands for thought, the breath of life and the wind through the trees, and for dealing with communication and the power of the mind.

Fire represents desire as well as connecting with strong will. Fire as energy in its natural form creates phenomena such as lightning and volcanoes, and of course there's man-made fire to warm ourselves with and to cook our food.

Water is the element of emotions and stability or grounding. In spiritual terms it is constantly flowing, used for healing, cleansing and purification. It is also associated with unconditional love.

Earth is stability, the ground beneath our feet. It represents our physical form, our flesh, blood, bones and hair.

We have many sayings related to these associations, such as, 'the cool breeze of reason', 'flames of passion', 'swamped by emotion' and 'solid as a rock'.

They also say that 'believing is not always seeing' and so it is with the angels of air because, just like magic, they can't be seen. The element of air is powerful as it provides oxygen for all living beings on Earth. Its symbol is a pair of wings, denoting communication, freedom, mental power and the intellect; the wings are significant in magic as they represent everything spiritual and the heavenly realms, which is why angels are depicted with wings.

Air is every breath we take as well as the wind that blows, causing the energies of our weather to flow across the world. In one moment it can give us the beautiful feeling of a soft breeze on our faces. But, as we have all seen, air can also be destructive, in the form of storms and even hurricanes and tornadoes.

Air is related to the soul and the powers of the mind and, as such, the angels of air are believed to help dispel any negativity from memories of past lives, assisting us to bring new ideas to fruition as well as recognising fresh opportunities that come our way. The archangel associated with the air is Raphael, who will assist us with spirituality in all its forms.

I myself had a past life regression with David, a friend of mine who is a medium, and prior to the session I asked Archangel Raphael to protect me at all times by offering his emerald green healing ray of light. Although I trust David implicitly, I was a little apprehensive as I wasn't sure which past life would present itself! I needn't have worried, it was an amazing experience and I felt safe throughout.

So if you need help or guidance with issues that may arise from a past life, call on Archangel Raphael to accompany you. A beautiful ritual that we can carry out in our own homes is that of 'the Angel Bells', which welcomes the angels of air and the elementals of that realm. We will need a set of wind chimes or hanging bells that create a tinkling noise when rung. If possible, try to get them in the shape of angels but if this isn't possible then any attractive chimes will do.

We hang them outside and ring them gently three times, calling on the angels of air to bless our homes. Wait for a while and, before long, the breeze will take the chimes and ring them in reply. This is a message from the angels to let you know your prayer has been heard and answered.

Now think of all the ways in which fire is beautiful in our lives, such as creating a romantic glow of warmth as we light a fire or candles at home. We use fire to entertain us too, with fireworks, bonfires and holding sparklers in our hands on Guy Fawkes Night. However, fire can also cause devastation by consuming everything within its path so must be strictly controlled.

Archangel Michael is the leader of the angels of fire who are strong and brave and will stand boldly at our side in times of trouble, shock or disturbance. Another way in which the angels of fire can assist us is by helping us to transform our lives, protecting us as we go through the changes that are necessary to reach our future goals.

The element of fire helps us with setting goals. A wonderful way to put this into action is to take a pen and paper and make a list of everything we are not happy about in life or in a particular situation. Then draw a line through these and make a new list of positive dreams and desires. Add a touch of magic to this by changing it into a letter to the elemental angels of fire, perhaps adding some colour or angelic images to it. Date and sign it, put it away... and watch what happens!

Let your worries wash away with the help of the angels of water for, as water flows, so does the mind, constantly evolving, adapting and growing. Simply by being in or near water can make us feel calmer and happier, with definite healing benefits from soaking in a warm bath or hot tub or swimming in the sea. Even listening to water can help us feel peaceful, such as being near a waterfall and hearing the sounds of the cascade, sitting by a fountain in the garden or on a beach. Relaxing music that includes sounds of the sea or the patter of rain can be beneficial for body and mind too.

The angels of water appear in feminine form because water is a feminine energy and connected with aspects of the goddess, so it's no surprise that Archangel Gabriel is believed by me, and many others, to be the angel of the element of water.

The water angels are, just like the seas, strong and pure and deep and they will help us to promote harmony from within. If we want a change of image in any way or to improve our self-image, they will help us to change how we feel about ourselves by giving us the willpower to go ahead and have a makeover. They are magical beings and can help with any kind of water magic we practise, such as using crystal bowls, invoking the seas or rivers, rains or mists. There are also various forms of divination using the tools of water, such as floatation, dowsing and scrying.

I used water scrying for the first time when I was co-host of the TV show *Rescue Mediums* and we went to a house that had been full of unexplained activity. My co-host Jackie and I found a large bowl into which we poured clear water, and inwardly spoke to our spirit guides as well as asking Archangel Gabriel to give us guidance. We dimmed the lights and held a candle carefully over the water.

As I concentrated, I saw that the water was starting to become cloudy and I could see hazy images. Eventually, these images became stronger and I was surprised by what I could clearly see and therefore convey. The information we gleaned from this form of water magic helped greatly with our psychic investigation, and I know that I had the angels of water by my side giving me encouragement, strength and belief in my abilities.

A great way to connect with the angels of water is to take a leisurely shower and, as you wash yourself, visualise a beautiful angel dressed in white standing under a magnificent healing waterfall. She beckons you to join her under the cascading water and, as you do so, you instantly feel the benefit of the water's cleansing and purifying energy. She hands you a pink lotus flower for love and a white rose for purity, clarity and beauty. She says that she will help to cleanse away any unhappy memories or neglected emotions in your life so that you are ready to make a fresh start. As the image of the angel starts to fade, remember to thank her. And when you step out of the shower, notice how relaxed and nourished you feel.

Earth is the land beneath our feet and when we go for a walk amongst nature we can always ask the angels of the earth to accompany us. I see the element of earth as the symbol of Mother Nature herself as it's nurturing, yet also solid and firm. For example, think about the beautiful trees and flowers you may see on a daily basis as well as thinking about the plants that feed and shelter us. The angels of the earth offer us security and stability and symbolise physical power and the maternal element of fertility.

Traditionally, the angel of the element of earth is Archangel Uriel who leads the angels of earth to help with natural disasters such as volcanoes, floods or avalanches. These angels will help us to feel grounded as we connect with the wisdom of our souls, and they are especially protective of those who are highly sensitive and who put others before themselves as they always want to help people feel happy no matter what. The term that is often used to describe these empathic, loving individuals is 'earth angels'.

Connect with the angels of earth by meditating outside on a warm day with bare feet and really feel at one with the earth energy as you ground and align with Mother Nature. If you wish, you could say the following prayer:

> *"Dear Archangel Uriel and the elemental angels of earth,*
> *thank you for guiding me to embrace my uniqueness*
> *and to believe in my dreams.*
> *Please help me to shine my light out to others*
> *to help them to love themselves and make the right decisions,*
> *as I believe in my own inner strength."*

The term 'earth angel' was coined by Doreen Virtue and a similar term often used is 'light worker'. Such people have become more recognised due to the shifts in energy and higher consciousness since the year 2000, when universal energy was speeded up. This affected spiritual souls so much that many felt their lives were literally out of control. Step forward, the new order of earth angels! One of their most important characteristics is that they themselves are often overlooked, as they choose to listen to others rather than be the centre of attention themselves. Then, no matter what is going on in their own lives, they will be there in an instant if others need to hear caring and comforting words, advice from the heart and loving guidance.

The celestial realms choose their earth angels wisely and a strong guardian angel is assigned to each one. Born to help make the world a better place, earth angels will often be placed in a dysfunctional family and will feel 'the odd one out' until they hear the angels' call. A certain event in their life may strike a chord which leads to them understanding their soul's purpose in life.

Sounds easy? Well, it isn't. The earth angel will be the one who has had to endure many obstacles on their life's path and has often been abused, put upon, bullied or ignored. However, when they hear the angels' call, they will be there to share their light with others as they finally step out onto centre stage and come into their own. They were born to bring light into what can often be a dark, depressing world and, as such, at some point in their lives they will transform just like a butterfly as it emerges from the chrysalis resplendent in beautiful colourful wings. It may be difficult to comprehend at first that the person before us surrounded by a beautiful glow used to be the brunt of bullying at school or were so shy they preferred their own company to that of others.

Do you recognise yourself here? One of the best ways in which to determine whether you are an earth angel is to ask Archangel Uriel to step forward and help you write down how you have felt all your life, from your early days to the present time, and how these emotions have stayed with you throughout. Doing this will assist in recognising and releasing long-term negative energy as Uriel helps you to find a happy balance in your life, in readiness for your spiritual transformation.

For example, have you always absorbed other people's energy and emotions? Have you always felt 'different', were you bullied or blamed for things you hadn't done? Do people treat you so badly that you feel as if your heart would break? And do you find it difficult to set healthy boundaries for yourself? You may have had an unhappy or unsettling childhood, or hated school as you were never one of the popular kids. All of these are signs of being an earth angel.

But it's not all doom and gloom! You will also delight in the beauty and magic around you, such as the aura around trees, the mystical full moon, the song of the birds and the flowers that grow against all odds in the most barren of places. So, if you could wave a magic wand and make a wish, would you want to heal the world? If so, then you are most definitely an earth angel and there will come a time in your life when you will find your true divine purpose as you spread your love, light and joy into the world.

A really good way to make a stronger connection with the elemental angels is by working with crystals, formed naturally below the Earth's surface. The process starts when water near the surface of the Earth starts to cool and harden, causing crystals to solidify ('crystallisation'). During this process, no two crystals are exactly the same in colour or size and each one links to the elements of earth, fire, water and air and to the corresponding angels.

The crystals that help us to connect with the element of earth are grounding stones that strengthen the mind and physical body. Examples of these are black tourmaline, obsidian, red jasper, smoky quartz and haematite.

The element of fire influences the reproductive and digestive systems, and the crystals of fire will help us to locate and shine our own light from within. These are tiger's eye, malachite, citrine and carnelian topaz.

The crystals of water are rose quartz, aquamarine, blue lace agate and larimar. The element of water is associated with the emotional mind and body and it helps us with communication and love for the self as well as for others.

As air is the element of our mental emotions, it is linked with all things spiritual and the letting go of negative emotions. Its crystals are amethyst, lapis lazuli, moonstone and selenite.

Many people have a selection of crystals that are placed in the home or a special one that is carried around with them, each infused with its own magical vibration and none more so than those that help us feel closer to the angels.

How to choose the crystal that is best for us? Close your eyes and ask the angels to help guide you towards the crystal that is meant for you. When you open your eyes, see which crystal seems the most prominent. If you cannot decide between two or three crystals, it's a good idea to hold each one in turn, feeling and sensing their energy and healing vibration. The one that calls out to you in terms of its warmth, healing energies or by a tingling in your hand is the one. And by the way, many wonderful crystals are usually readily available and not too expensive.

Before working with any new crystal, it will need to be cleansed and charged. Wash it in lightly salted water or in the sea, and then place it outside during the day although not when the sun is extremely hot. You will not want to start a fire, as the crystal focuses the sun's light, or have your crystal fade in colour, which can happen with amethyst or citrine. Do place your crystal outside overnight so that it can be charged in the moonlight.

Ensure that the crystal is only handled by you. If someone else picks it up or handles it in any way, you will have to go through the ritual of cleansing it all over again!

However, there are certain crystals that should not be cleansed by washing them such as selenite which is water soluble and layered crystals such as the beautiful angel wing calcite. Further, if you feel parts of the crystal might break away if it is cleansed in water, then don't do so. And if you do use salt to cleanse your crystal, ensure that you brush off every trace of the salt once it has been charged as this could damage the stone.

Once a crystal has been cleansed and charged, ideally it should be placed on an angel altar beside an angel figurine for at least twenty-four hours. This simple rite reinforces our intention of being ready to work with our angel crystal. Once blessed by the angels, the crystal may be kept on the altar or carried around in a pocket or purse so that we have the energy of the angels with us at all times. However, if it comes into contact with coins we shall need to cleanse our crystal again because money is handled by many other people. Ideally, place the crystal in a satin or velvet bag.

Holding our special crystal when meditating is also a wonderful way of connecting with the angels, as is placing it by our bed to promote positive dreams. Amethyst is a great stone to hold during meditation for connecting with angelic energy, especially if we are only just starting out developing our intuition.

It's a protective stone around the home, too, particularly if placed in the busiest room in the house, often the kitchen. Amethyst is also known as the dream stone, and if placed under your pillow it can help to promote pleasant dreams and brings about spiritual abundance.

If we want to be especially close to the angels, then angel aura quartz is a beautiful stone. It can help in awakening our spiritual awareness as it heals any inhibitions we may have about our worth. It's also a great stress reliever, as it releases negative emotional issues, transmuting them into positivity and peace.

A readily available and lovely angelic crystal is celestite, coloured blue and often with flecks of white here and there. It's the crystal used for the highest connection and attunement to the angelic realms. Golden rutilated quartz is usually clear in appearance yet with what looks like angel hair inclusions inside it in a golden colour, hence the name. It's a magical stone that helps to release any blockages that are holding us back.

Kunzite, representing unconditional love, and hiddenite, for healing and new beginnings, are transparent or translucent crystals that not only help us connect with divine energy on all levels but are safe, soft and gentle. They especially help those who suffer from depression or low self-esteem. Similarly, the beautiful white crystal selenite imbues positive energy so when placed in a bedroom it will emanate serenity and a calm ambience, raising our consciousness in order to connect with the celestial realms.

Saving perhaps the best until last, seraphinite is a gorgeous crystal that is olive green with white streaks which can often look like angelic feathers or angel wings. Naturally, the angelic name of this crystal means 'the Seraphim' who are one of the highest orders within the hierarchy of angels. This is a healing stone, allowing the owner to connect with the highest angelic realms – but only when they are fully ready to do so. It is not one to use for those only just starting out on the path of connecting with the angels as it is extremely powerful.

10
Angel magic

"The magic of angels abounds with love."
(The author)

Before meditation or, indeed, any spiritual work, we should always be grounded as it's essential to protect our physical bodies while trying to live a spiritual life. This is important so that we are not drained by negative energy that may be around us. Grounding and psychic protection are not just good practice for mediums or healers, they are things that everyone should get used to doing as a way of keeping our feet firmly on the ground and protecting our personal aura.

Those who ignore or forget about this may feel unbalanced or lethargic, generally unwell, not to mention the possibility of picking up others' emotional trauma. It can feel as if they are going around in circles, their heads full of clutter, they are overemotional or anxious, their senses totally disconnected as though they are not in control of their own lives.

Yet this daily ritual is easy to do, in order to feel focused and mindful. We certainly feel the difference afterwards, loving ourselves and spiritually aware. We will be energised and balanced and will notice that we don't feel drained around certain people any more. The best time to perform a grounding ritual is first thing in the morning so that we're protected for the rest of the day.

Find a quiet, peaceful place, close the eyes and concentrate on breathing, slowing it down with each breath taken. When you're ready, visualise thick, sturdy roots like those of a tree growing from the soles of your feet and send them down into the Earth until you feel centred. Imagine pure white light coming up from the Earth through the feet and bring it up through your body so you are filled with divine light. Now visualise a golden orb of light over the top of your head that opens and sends down golden light around the outside of your body from the top of your head right down to your feet until you are totally cocooned in a bubble of healing light.

For double protection, we can visualise putting on Archangel Michael's blue cloak of protection. This divine cloak of light has a hood, fastens securely, has long sleeves and reaches the ground. Then we should thank the angels, ready to start our day with their divine love and protection.

One of the most powerful tools we can use when connecting with the angels is that of beautiful fragrances in the form of pure essential oils; these are derived from plant extracts and have been used throughout history in many different cultures and religions. An example of this is during ancient Egyptian times when resins and herbs such as sandalwood, myrrh, thyme, cinnamon and coriander were used in healing practices, and the essence of water lilies was associated with rebirth.

Nowadays, we can benefit from adding a few drops of our favourite oil to an oil burner in order to help boost our mood, help us get a better night's sleep and, of course, deepen our connection to the angels who help create a positive flow of energy throughout our home and personal space. There really isn't a better ambience for feeling the love and light of the angels around us as we inhale the beautiful scent of our favourite aromatherapy oil during prayer or meditation.

Which oil to use when asking the angels for help? It's always best to choose one that we love the scent of ourselves, one that makes us feel at peace. The angels want us to feel happy and comfortable when connecting with them. If we feel that we have to burn a specific oil in order to connect with our guardian angels, even though we dislike its scent, this really won't help activate the connection between us!

On the other hand, many believe that certain fragrances are associated with specific angels, and a lovely one to use when connecting with guardian angels – as long as we like the aroma – is rose geranium. For Archangel Michael, the 'king of oils' frankincense is a good choice for focus, protection and learning spiritual truths. For Archangel Gabriel, some choose the essential oil of lemon to help them make better decisions, whilst rosemary help us lift our mood and trust the wisdom from within when reaching out to Archangel Uriel. For Archangel Jophiel, basil is a good choice as it makes us feel more cheerful and balances the mind, body and soul. To connect with Archangel Raphael, lavender is the best oil for healing and harmonious energy.

Our relationship with the angels is enhanced by having certain items around the home, or carried on our person, that remind us of the celestial realms such as crystals, an angel figurine, a piece of jewellery with angel wings or angel pictures on the wall. Angel oracle cards can also bring much comfort and guidance. Even when we are only just starting to learn about the angels, we can pick a card a day or whenever we feel the need for a little angelic assistance. When choosing a deck, ask the angels to guide you to the perfect one for you and notice how you feel on all levels, about the illustrations, messages and description on the box. Very often a deck of cards will seem to 'call' to us, the angels' way of letting us know it's the right one.

Any new deck of cards needs to be cleansed before we use it. A simple way to do this is to take the cards out of the box and cleanse them by visualising a golden light around the deck. Then ask the angels to bless them as you hold each card in turn, to blend your energy with theirs. Hold the cards in a fan shape over your heart chakra and say,

> *"Dear angels, please infuse these cards
> with the purest light and allow my energy
> to flow through them with divine blessings for all.
> Thank you."*

To come even closer to the angels, we can place the deck under our pillow as we sleep at night. I have come to believe that by having my deck of cards so close they will offer me protection from negative energy, as well as helping me with my readings, whether for myself or others.

When I bought one particular deck, for example, the cards felt stiff and even though I cleansed them as I normally do they didn't feel right. So I took them out of the box (which also felt quite sterile), put them in a handmade velvet pouch and placed them under my pillow to help me bond with them. Before I went to sleep, I asked the angels to bless my cards. It was the best night's sleep I'd had in ages!

It can happen that after a while an oracle deck can feel a little 'stagnant'. Perhaps they are a little tired or 'out of sorts' if they've not been used for a while, if they've been picked up by someone else or if we have done a reading for a particularly negative person.

If so, they can then be recharged by tapping each card in the deck gently. Alternatively, we can smudge the deck with our favourite incense in order to cleanse the energy of the cards. We hold the deck of cards a little higher than the smoking incense as we swirl the smoke over each card in turn, asking the angels to bless them in readiness for us working with them again. We do this three times, thank the angels, and place the deck on top of our angel altar for three days with a cleansed piece of clear quartz on top of the cards.

If you are a Reiki practitioner, you can give this special energy healing to your cards. Others like to use the magic of the full moon by shuffling the cards a few times then putting the deck on a cloth made of natural fibre such as cotton, placed on a flat surface directly under the natural beauty of the full moon.

When cared for well, oracle cards really do possess an energy of their own. We can see this sometimes when cards literally 'jump' out of a deck when shuffling them and thinking about a question we need an answer to. This is when the angels are drawing our attention to the cards that will be the most significant for us at that particular time. If this ever happens for you, please don't ignore your jumping cards as it's my belief they offer important messages.

Over the years I have given many mediumistic readings for clients. As many other people who carry out readings will agree, the information given to a client is not retained by the reader. We do not keep any record of the content because the information is not ours. Moreover, apart from it being very personal to the client, it can often be very draining especially when picking up on negative or heart-rending information. So I asked a few of my clients (names changed to protect their privacy) to share their stories of having angel readings with me.

Peter spoke from his heart.

"It was such a profound experience. You brought my wife so much peace and her faith was restored. You may remember that, at the time, her Dad had passed away and she was devastated, her pain was so immense. However, with the angels' help, you described his personality perfectly. You picked up on his amputations, something that no-one other than us knew about, and the crazy way he used to take his teeth in and out to scare the local children, although it had the opposite effect as they just jumped up and down asking him to do it all over again!

"Your angel cards were something else. Each one confirmed all that was going on in our lives at the time and you gave us some future information, too, that has now come true. For example, you told us that we would be moving house and that it would be very special indeed in an unusual way. We found our new home and the vibe was so uplifting that we fell in love with it, prayed it stayed on the market for us which it did and we were soon moving in. What we didn't know at first was how spot on you were about the special qualities of our new home. We eventually found out that it was the former home of Phil Collins who had lived there with his family."

Andrew reminded me that a few years ago he had sunk into a "dark hole" and contemplated suicide.

"Everything around me that could go wrong went wrong, and I found myself trying to survive from one minute to the next. I hurt so badly that I lost my psychic ability and my sensitivity, which was heartbreaking as my spirituality has always been my life. I also lost all my savings due to a bad decision over the years and I only saw myself as a failure.

"My partner suggested I spoke to Alison for help and, when I did, she noticed straight away there was something wrong and that I needed help. She offered to connect with me remotely via video link to help me. Week after week she would call me to take me through a healing process with the angels and was drawn to angel cards that were so salient I couldn't believe it at first. Yet the information was there, particularly from Archangel Michael, about cord-cutting. Alison never charged me for her help as she was told by the angels not to, for they knew how 'on the edge' I felt. She offered her time and patience to give of herself when she was going through difficulties herself.

"Despite all the obstacles, I eventually regained myself and am now a practising medium with international clients. Alison and her angels knew how to approach my situation to help realign my energy, mind and emotions. From feeling hopeless, I now trust her implicitly and value her as a dear friend. Alison has proved that angels do indeed exist."

Patricia remembered being nervous when she came for an angel card reading with me.

"But she soon put me at my ease. During my reading she looked up from her cards and said a blessing was to make its way to me and my husband and she saw a baby in the arms of a loved one in the spirit world. She said it was a baby to be born. After many IVF treatments I had all but lost hope. Yet soon afterwards I found out I was pregnant and then gave birth to the most perfect little girl."

When I gave a reading to Sandy, one of the messages that kept being repeated throughout from two different decks of angel cards was not to ignore the synchronous signs and omens being sent her way. These would particularly be in the form of angel numbers in a repetitive sequence. This lady had been keeping all her emotions bottled up within, having been hurt by someone recently, and said she hadn't noticed any number signs. However, she said she would try her best to be ever-present from now on so as not to miss them. Later that week I received a message from her.

"Dear Alison, I just had to tell you that I've followed the advice that came through in the reading you gave me very closely and today I took a huge step forward! I tried to be brave but still cried a little, as it's not easy for me to say how I really feel sometimes. Here's my grocery receipt from yesterday and you can see 5555 in angel numbers! It can't be clearer, can it? And it all started with the reading with you and those beautiful angel cards."

Indeed, I looked at the photograph she'd sent of her grocery receipt and it put a big smile on my face as the last three amounts were all 55.55. This predicts a period of spiritual awakening and transformative personal growth – a powerful message.

I have mentioned how valuable an angelic altar can be in our homes as a wonderful way to feel close to the angels. It is a place dedicated to connecting with the angels, helping us to express ourselves emotionally, spiritually and mentally. It's a portal to serenity. The altar will emanate peace and tranquillity within the home because each item chosen by us to stand on our altar has been charged with our energy and love.

The first home altars were used as far back as at least Neolithic times. Although these items and the altars themselves might have been fairly crude affairs compared to those we use nowadays, this does not detract from those people's belief in otherworldly beings of love and light. They lovingly made each artefact themselves out of stone, flint, wood and bones, to pay homage to those in other dimensions. Many of these items that have been excavated, such as carvings and artefacts of angelic spirits dating back thousands of years, are on display in museums all over the world.

Such altars would often have been dedicated to fertility gods and goddesses, such as Ishtar, the ancient goddess of love (and war!). Ishtar was worshipped from the beginning of recorded history and her name varied from one continent to another, becoming more widely known as Aphrodite or Venus, the goddess of love and beauty. Many scholars believe that she began as a simple Neolithic fertility goddess but then gradually assumed the role of 'the mother goddess'.

An altar does not have to be large but it should be in a special place where we can be alone and undisturbed. Having decided this, the altar should be blessed by anointing it with an essential oil such as lavender. This ritual is called 'altar devotion' as we are literally devoting the altar to the unconditional love of the angels by cleansing and preparing it before placing angelic artefacts on its blessed surface. We can then say a positive mantra such as:

> *"I dedicate this altar to the celestial beings.*
> *May the angels enter my home and life*
> *as they help me make positive changes*
> *and increase my spirituality.*
> *May my guardian angel continue to speak to me*
> *and allow me to connect with the voices of all angels.*
> *So mote it be."*

White, gold or silver candles are an essential part of any altar as they emit a magic of their own. Then each time we connect with the angels in our special place, we light the candle(s) and ask the angels to step forward. Anything else we choose to place on the altar should be things that remind us of angelic love and energy, such as figurines, pictures, jewellery, fresh flowers, cleansed crystals and angel cards.

We then charge each item before adding it to the altar by holding it in our left hand and cupping our right hand over it. Now sit with eyes closed for a moment and imagine a golden light around the item, asking the angels to bless it and feeling the warmth of it in our hands.

Whilst having a permanent altar in our home is ideal, these days we are often travelling. So if we are away from home from time to time, a temporary altar is better than none. Just take a few items along, perhaps a small candle, a figurine and a crystal, and remember to bless the place you put them with a little essential oil.

Many people even create 'subliminal' altars around their homes without realising it. For example, these could be beautiful arrangements of photographs, plants, flowers and ornaments that have been lovingly placed together, giving a feeling of peace and positive energy in that area.

Edith Wharton said, "There are two ways of spreading light: be the candle or the mirror that reflects it." Yes, candles have a magic of their own and their flame helps to amplify positive energy around our homes and personal spaces. The angels are particularly drawn to the flame of a candle as it enhances the effects of our prayers through the element of fire.

We can go one step further, communicating with a specific angel by choosing a candle in the colour that corresponds with them.

For example, a white candle denotes purity, communication, peace and healing, and the angel associated with this is Archangel Gabriel, angel of the white ray of light. On the other hand, a gold candle stands for power, abundance and success, and is one of the highest vibrational colours of the angelic realm, associated with the Christ consciousness. Similarly, the Christ light is invoked by a silver candle, strengthening our intuition and calling for divine purity.

If you feel drawn to a purple or violet candle, you are looking for spirituality, insight, mercy and change. Reach out to

Archangel Zadkiel, angel of the violet flame of transmutation. A blue candle represents protection, strength, courage and truth, associated with Archangel Michael of the blue ray, whereas the candle for good fortune or healing would be green and linked with Archangel Raphael.

The colour pink focuses the mind on relationships, nurturing and divine love, and calls to Archangel Chamuel, the angel of love. It's Archangel Jophiel who responds to a yellow candle, which denotes joy, abundance, clarity and beauty. The angel of empowerment is Archangel Metatron, so if we are looking for personal growth and freedom we choose an orange candle. A red candle, however, stands for wisdom, passion and intimacy and is linked with the angel of wisdom, Archangel Uriel.

It may surprise some to know that a black candle is very protective and helps to banish negativity by transmuting it into safety and protection. We can call on any or all of the angels by using a black candle. Of course, it is also often used with magical spells.

Angels breathe their divine love into us human beings and all living things from birds, insects and animals to trees and flowers. Just think of how we feel good to be alive as we walk through a garden or a park full of the most beautiful flowers, enjoying their colour, beauty and scent. It's so uplifting and helps pour loving energy into our day in such a natural way. We can bring the magic of nature into our homes too, with aromatherapy oils and plants or cut flowers, even on or beside our altars.

Some plants have long been associated with divine energy, such as honeysuckle for its wonderful scent, and this gorgeous plant represents peacefulness, mindfulness and positivity, inviting the angels of love to draw close. Jasmine is one of my own favourite scents and I have this 'lady of the night' bush in my garden, its aroma swirling within and outside the home during summer evenings. This plant helps to feed the birds and the delicate hummingbird moths, which are a joy to behold, and its scent often accompanies my guardian angel Mya as she enters.

The name 'lavender' is derived from the Latin *lavare* which means 'to wash' so it is used when bathing, to freshen linen and drawers, to soothe headaches and help relaxation and sleep. Lavender is calming and healing and is therefore used to treat many conditions such as burns, wounds, acne, eczema, insomnia, anxiety and even hair loss as well as helping us overcome emotional challenges by transmuting negative energy into positive. The angel associated with lavender is Archangel Zadkiel, the angel of the violet ray of transmutation.

Lilies are associated with Archangel Gabriel because, it is said, she held a lily in her hand as she appeared before the Virgin Mary, to denote her purity. This flower is also known as the flower of fertility and rebirth. Further, the key to emotional rebirth, lightness of spirit and transformation is the primrose with its joyful, bright face, and the angel associated with this plant is Archangel Uriel, the angel of wisdom. This was, apparently, Queen Victoria's favourite flower.

Roses are, of course, known as 'the queen of flowers' as they have a special beauty of their own, from their scent, colour and symbolic meaning throughout history. There have been stories, poems and songs written about roses for centuries and they have always been associated with the celestial worlds because of the purity and love in their petals. Angels will often leave a scent of roses as a sign of their presence because the flower has a much higher energy frequency than any other on the Earth. The angel that is most associated with the rose is Archangel Barachiel.

"Love is a flower, you've got to let it grow," sang John Lennon in *Mind Games*. The natural beauty of flowers helps us all to feel the angels' love.

I have often mentioned the 'magic' of angels and everyone deserves a little magic in their lives… so here are a few angel spells, each one unique, safe and yet powerful in its own way. Working with spells is all about having the right intentions and, when we have love in our hearts and want to help other people, the angels will step in and assist.

Knot spells, or cord magic, have been practised for thousands of years in ancient Greece, Egypt and Babylon. Knots would be tied or untied for many purposes such as handfasting, protection, love and change. Sailors have traditionally tied and untied three knots, believing that the angels (or witches!) would 'sell the wind' to them: the first knot helped to create a gentle wind, the second a strong wind and the third would bring a powerful storm.

We bind a spell initially by tying knots in ribbon and then we release the spell as the knots are untied. An angel knot spell is powerful yet fairly easy to cast, even for beginners. Choose a ribbon in either white, gold or silver, the colours representing the angelic realm, and light the candles on your angel altar. You are going to ask the angels for their divine guidance in something you need help with.

We make nine knots in the ribbon, holding it up with the first knot in the centre. The second knot is to the left of that one, the third to the right of the centre knot, and then we repeat this action alternately. All the while, we are thinking of what we want the angels to help us with by saying a chosen prayer. Everyone can choose their own words as this will strengthen the creative spark and help us get even closer to the angels, or use this spell:

> "As I tie knot one, this spell has begun.
> As I tie knot two, my dreams will ensue.
> As I tie knot three, I feel happy and free.
> As I tie knot four, my desires are secure.
> Now knot five is done, my worry has gone.
> Now knot six is done, my life's full of fun.
> By the knot of seven, I connect with angels in Heaven.
> By the knot of eight, I believe in good fate.
> By the knot of nine, love and protection are mine.
> So mote it be."

We place the knotted ribbon on our altar or carry it around with us until we feel happier and the angels have transmuted our issue into positivity. Then we untie the knots, thank the angels for their divine assistance, and keep the ribbon in a chosen place of peace and tranquillity in our home.

Banishing spells have also been used for centuries. Pagans, for example, would cast such a spell to get rid of either a person or a situation that didn't serve them. If we use such a spell while working with the angels, it becomes more effective, safe and will harm no-one.

Find a small box in either purple or lilac, or decorate one yourself to make it even more magical. Write down what, or who, it is that you want to get rid of – perhaps a person who has harmed you by bullying, stalking or by being abusive – state their name and ask the angels to banish them from your life in a safe way. You may wish to invoke Archangel Michael in particular, the warrior and protector. Put the paper inside your box and seal it. You will find, with trust and belief in your heart, that this person will move on from your life in a natural way.

An angel wings spell is easy to do and we only need to draw and cut out a pair of angel wings on white card. Then we write on them whatever we need to, such as affirmations, dreams, our wishes or problems, before asking our guardian angel for their loving guidance. If we have written positive affirmations on our angel wings, they can be placed on our angel altar or anywhere else in the home where we will see them often. On the other hand, if the message describes a negative situation, we should then burn the wings safely outdoors, saying a mantra such as:

> *"I am grateful to my heavenly guardian angel*
> *for being by my side as they deal with this problem.*
> *This spell is done, it begins right now.*
> *So mote it be."*

Finally, I can vouch that certain clients have found this fertility spell to work! Having properly grounded ourselves, we gather together a picture of Archangel Gabriel, the angel of fertility and the elemental angel of water, and place a small bowl of water with a cleansed piece of moonstone or selenite next to it. In front of the bowl, light a white candle. We say the following prayer, repeating the ritual for the next seven days:

> *"Beloved Archangel Gabriel of the white ray of light,*
> *please bless [names] with the love and light of your divinity*
> *by helping [them/us] to believe and know*
> *that the dream of bearing a perfect child will become true.*
> *May this child be conceived as a beautiful gift of love*
> *as soon as possible.*
> *Trusting in your presence always and thanking you*
> *for sending this child, we are happy in knowing*
> *that this request has already been answered.*
> *Thank you, beloved Archangel Gabriel. It is done."*

11
Meditation and prayer

"Quiet the mind and the soul will speak."
(Ma Jaya Sati Bhagavati)

First, a gentle reminder to ensure that we are grounded and aligned before any spiritual practice, as described earlier. I repeat this because it's so important to release any negative energy we may have unknowingly gathered earlier in the day. We should choose a peaceful place where we won't be disturbed and, when we feel relaxed, we close our eyes and concentrate on our breathing.

If we are holding on to negative thoughts or worries, we bring that energy down through the body from the top of the head and visualise it seeping out through the soles of the feet, right down into the rich soil of Mother Earth. Now, in order to connect ourselves to the core of the Earth, we think of ourselves as rooted, as if by thick and sturdy tree roots, deeply into the Earth. Some people may even experience a slight 'pull', which confirms their grounding, but don't worry if you don't feel it.

In order to protect our aura, or energy field, we can visualise a ball of energy over the top of our crown that opens up and sends a beautiful ethereal white light down through the body. Now visualise a perfect golden light coming down from the angelic kingdom and swirling around the outside of the body. So we are cocooned in golden light, one of the highest vibrational colours of the angelic realm.

For even greater protection, you may like to visualise putting on Archangel Michael's blue ray cloak of light. See it as a cloak that reaches down to the ground, has long sleeves and a hood covering the head.

Over time and with experience, you will be able to create your own methods of grounding and aligning as you will know what suits you best in fully protecting your energy.

The practice of meditation is magical and at the heart of all things spiritual. So whether you are a beginner or more advanced, the following meditations will help you connect with the angels at a pace that is right for you. After grounding, invoke your guardian angel and ask them to be present as you journey within.

If you are going to follow the guided meditations, a good idea is to record them on your phone so that you can focus fully on the words. Alternatively, if you meditate in a group then one person could read the meditations straight from this book. You may also like to share these meditations with family or friends then discuss your experiences together. It's also helpful to write them down in a journal, so each time you meditate you can see how far you have come in connecting with divine energy.

Finally, for those of you who have hearing difficulties, do read the meditations several times in order to form a clear idea of their themes within your mind. This will then enable you to enjoy the practice on your own terms with the divine guidance of your guardian angel. And for those of you who have sight problems, ask a family member or a dear friend to guide you through the meditations.

Some people like to listen to relaxing music that has an angelic quality while they meditate, helping them to feel calm, and nowadays there is so much to choose from. For example, there are classical pieces such as Ennio Morricone's *Gabriel's Oboe* or Debussy's *La Mer*, or New Age spiritual music composed by people like Llewellyn (*Journey to the Angels, Crystal Angels*), David Wright (*Prophecy*) and Clifford White (*Ascension*). Another idea is to listen to nature sounds such as waves, rainfall or birdsong, anything that can help you feel closer to the angels.

This first meditation is a great one for beginners as it helps to strengthen each of the psychic senses of clairvoyance, clairaudience, clairsentience and claircognisance, each helping us to get even closer to the angels. Start with your feet firmly on the ground and hands on knees, and concentrate on your breathing: inhale deeply, hold for a count of three, then slowly exhale, imagining that you are releasing anything that no longer serves you. Do this until you feel relaxed and at one with yourself.

❖ The journey begins by visualising yourself sitting on dry, springy grass by a softly running stream. You watch it trickle over large stones and you enjoy the gentle noise it makes. You feel calm and peaceful, enjoying being in the moment. Close your eyes and notice what other noises you hear. When you open your eyes, take a good look around. What do you see? Notice how you are feeling. Enjoy having some time just for yourself.

You touch the grass and enjoy the sensation of it beneath your hands. Overhead, birds are singing and you can hear the rustle of leaves on the nearby trees. It looks like the boughs of the trees are nodding to you and you walk over to a tree that you are drawn to and put your arms around it. Feel its loving energy as you sense absolute calm washing over you. Rub your hands gently on the rough surface of the bark and feel at one with nature.

You decide to go back to the stream as the running

water seems to be calling to you. Take off your shoes and, when you are barefoot, sit down and dip your feet into the water. It feels warm and inviting.

(Allow yourself to stay with this peaceful state for five or six minutes.)

When you are ready, step back into your room and feel the sensation of sitting back down on your chair as you bring your awareness back to the here and now. Wriggle your fingers and toes and, when you are ready, open your eyes. Take a drink of water.

The next meditation is to help you meet your guardian angel. Start by slowing your breath right down and letting go of any worries by focusing on the image of your favourite flower. Notice its colour and how pretty its petals are. You may even get a sense of its aroma or how it would feel if you were holding it. Now visualise a field full of your favourite flowers in every colour of the rainbow. See yourself there, in this stunning place. You may even want to run among the flowers, feeling free, happy and uplifted.

- ❖ Sit down on soft grass under the shade of an old oak tree, take a good look around and enjoy listening to the songbirds. You are perfectly safe here. When you are ready, ask your guardian angel to join you. Trust and believe that they can hear you, whether your request was said out loud or within your mind.

    After a short while you look up to the sky and watch how the clouds move around. One in particular forms in the shape of angel wings which intrigues you, especially when you see something floating down in front of you. It's not just one pure white feather, but three in succession and each one appears fluffy. When they are near enough, you catch them and notice how they feel in your hand.

Eventually you hear a sound to your left and you watch in awe as a ball of light appears, gradually getting brighter. The light makes you feel protected, comforted and loved in a way you've never felt before. It gets bigger and bigger until it moves in front of you and a figure forms within the light. And as the figure steps forward you realise that you are in the company of an angel.

Notice everything about them, from their beautiful wings that stretch out to the side to their facial features and hair. You realise in an instant that the three feathers you hold in your hand are from their wings and you thank your angel for this gift. As they stand before you, you feel so small, just like a child next to this tall, celestial being.

Your angel holds your face gently in their hands, and tell you that they will be with you forever. They invite you to ask them questions, anything you wish. They may even share their name with you. But don't worry if this doesn't happen, as they will share more about themselves each time you connect with them through patience and practice. In this moment, you realise how blessed you are. You feel perfectly safe and enjoy being in the company of your angel.

(Stay silent for five to ten minutes.)

Eventually, your angel folds their divine wings around you and you feel their softness and warmth. Just relax in the angel's wings for as long as you like, for time is irrelevant in the company of your own guardian angel. When their wings unfold, the light enfolds them once again and, as the light moves away to your left, you say goodbye to your angel.

Once they have gone, you realise that they have placed something in your hand, a stunning crystal that feels smooth in texture. You know without a doubt that in time you will find one just like it to add to your angel altar. In your other hand, you still hold the three white feathers.

As you retrace your steps back to the here and now, you can still feel the love and security of your angel's embrace. Please bring your awareness back now to the present time. Walk back into the room and feel the chair beneath you. Wriggle your fingers and toes and, when you are ready, open your eyes and notice how strong, determined and peaceful you feel. Take a drink of water.

Once you know that you have felt your guardian angel's presence, it's time to get to know them better! Start by reaching out to them as follows:

> *"Dear guardian angel caring for me,*
> *please be by my side by divine decree.*
> *Thank you helping me along the way.*
> *Protected by you, I keep worry at bay.*
> *Please take me on a journey of light,*
> *as I learn to trust with all my might."*

Have patience as your guardian angel steps forward to accompany you in this meditation.

- ❖ The journey begins as you visualise yourself stepping outside your home, to see before you a doorway, clear and shining in golden light. You feel it's a door to another world and you walk through it with your angel by your side, knowing you are perfectly safe. The scene before you now takes your breath away, as the most beautiful garden you have ever seen opens up and stretches as far as the eyes can see.

    The colours here are so bright and everything is enveloped in a glow that pulsates like a heartbeat. This garden is truly alive and is full of pure love, peace and serenity. As you look around you see something new, something different with each blink of an eye. There are musical fountains, flowers and plants in the most beautiful

MEDITATION AND PRAYER

shades of pink, blue, lavender and the purest white. Swans glide along a stream sparkling with silvery light, where cream water lilies bob up and down on the ebb and flow of the water. Tall marble angelic figurines guard an arbour surrounded in fairy lights, and ancient majestic trees are covered by flowers and luscious fruits.

Your guardian angel invites you to sit with them on comfortable cushions inside the arbour and you watch as more angels busy themselves by tending to the flowers, plants and animals that have come to join them in this garden of light.

Know that this is your special place, where you can talk to your angel just as you would a best friend, for that is what they are. Know that your angel has been assigned to you personally and they know you better than you know yourself. As you communicate with your angel, the bond between you will strengthen and will with experience allow you to find answers from within that you never thought possible. Allow your angel to help guide you towards your divine life purpose. Take this time to get to know your angel. You can ask them anything you wish. But have patience!

(Rest here and enjoy the peace for five or six minutes.)

Now it's time to come back to the present. Your angel guides you back through the doorway of golden light and you find yourself outside your home. Your angel hugs you tightly and you feel their divine love for you as you watch them walk away through the doorway.

Make your way back into the room where you started your journey. Take your time coming back to the here and now. Wriggle fingers and toes and only open your eyes when you are ready. Take a drink of water.

Alongside our guardian angel, we each have an animal spirit guide with special abilities to help us learn as we follow our spiritual path. We can call upon them for help and guidance at any time. First, let's meet them!

- Visualise yourself sitting beside a beautiful lake on a warm day. You watch a family of swans glide by as the sun glints on the water, and you feel good inside as you take in your tranquil surroundings. There are tall trees nearby, covered in scented blossom. Everything feels quiet and serene in this safe haven and you lean back against a tree and close your eyes, inwardly asking your guardian angel to come forward.

    You hear the sound of the birds singing and as you open your eyes a butterfly floats down and lands on your hand. Concentrate on the butterfly – what colour is it, how does it feel on your hand? It opens and closes its lovely delicate wings and, after a while, it flies off up and up into the sky until it's as small as a dot that finally disappears from view.

    Now you realise that you are not alone as you can see a pair of inquisitive eyes peeping at you from behind the trees. All becomes clear when an animal steps out and starts to walk slowly towards you. This is your angel animal guide and they are here to help you and give you strength. What kind of animal is it? Carefully notice its colour and form, the way it moves, the look in its eyes. It comes to sit at your feet and you pet your animal guide, feeling completely safe in their presence.

    In the distance you hear the sweet sound of a harp. It is so beautiful and seems to be on a different vibration as if it has come from a place of joy and purity. Then you hear soft choral singing accompanying the harp and you feel relaxed and at one with yourself and the world. Now a pure white glow appears before you, getting bigger and bigger

MEDITATION AND PRAYER

until eventually it takes the form of a very large angel, your guardian angel. Talk to them about anything, share your worries, for they are also here to give you healing.

(Enjoy these special moments with your guardian angel for five or six minutes.)

Your angel will give you a message. Remember what this is as it has come direct from the celestial realms and is sent with unconditional love. Soon it is time to leave your angel and your animal guide so say your goodbyes, but know that you can come back to the tranquil lake any time you wish to connect with your divine helpers.

When you are ready, please bring your awareness back into the room. Listen to the sounds around you, wriggle your fingers and toes and open your eyes when you are ready. Take a drink of water.

Now you know who your animal spirit guide is, look up their meaning. You may be surprised! How do you think they will be able to help you?

They say that "love is all you need" but life isn't that simple, is it? Whilst some are blessed with loving family and friends, for others there is loss and heartbreak. But the truth is that love is within us always and with the angels' guidance we can find it whenever we need to. Let's meet the angel of love…

❖ You start your journey in a delightful little square lined with cafés and orange trees in a quaint Mediterranean town. Notice what the people look like and what they are wearing. There is a happy vibe here and you feel warm and comfortable inside. Pause for a moment, listening to the natural sounds of the town, people talking to one another, someone whistling a familiar tune, the distant cry of a cockerel and the faint melodious sound of church bells.

On the other side of the square you see a cobbled street that curves upwards and you go to explore. Start walking along the street noticing how narrow it is and how pretty the whitewashed villas are, resplendent with window boxes full of brightly coloured flowers. As the path climbs higher, there are fewer villas and more trees. There are tall palm trees framed by the blue sky, and their fan-shaped leaves rustle in the warm breeze.

Eventually, you come to some white stone steps that you start to climb with steady determination. Reaching the top, you walk towards a majestic tree adorned with purple flowers, providing a shady area beside an ancient wishing well. Throw a coin into the clear water and make a wish.

(Pause for a few minutes.)

Now look up and notice a beautiful little church nestled in the mountains ahead of you. How did you not see it before? You look incredulously at this perfect scene of the stone church surrounded by orange and lemon trees. You catch the scent of the orange blossom and sigh happily as you realise you are the only person here – and yet you don't feel alone. You walk towards the church and notice that the door is open as though welcoming you. Inside, look around at the stained glass windows with the sun casting its beams of light around this haven of serenity. What else do you see?

(Pause for two or three minutes.)

It's not long before you see someone walking towards you, surrounded by a golden light and holding out their hands to you. You realise you are in the presence of a stunning angel and you feel elated as she approaches you and opens her wings, wrapping them around you in a loving embrace. She starts to sing gently to you and you have never heard a voice so pure and full of unconditional love. She tells you that she is one of the angels of love and you sit together on a pew.

(Enjoy this magical inner feeling for five or six minutes.)

It is time for you to leave. Say goodbye then start to walk back past the tree with purple flowers and the wishing well, until you come once again to the steps. Climbing down the steps you notice how serene you feel, all your worries have melted away. You turn to thank the angel and she blows you a kiss before fading into the distance.

Back on the cobbled path, notice what you see along the way until you finally arrive at the square. You hear the church bells ringing in the distance and smile to yourself. This is your very own magical space, somewhere that you can escape to alone any time you wish, whenever you need to feel that love, and it is your secret.

Bring your awareness back to the here and now, step back into your room, feel the chair beneath you and, when you are ready, open your eyes. Take a drink of water.

This meditation is particularly meaningful for me as it was extremely vivid in full colour and I really was there. Afterwards, I wrote the details down in my journal thinking to myself that I would love to go to somewhere like that, rustic, charming, natural and so relaxing. A couple of weeks later, my husband took me to the small town of Altea for the first time and there was the square I had seen in my meditation, exactly as I had seen it! There was the path leading up to a quaint blue and white church, the small villas with the most beautiful window boxes full of beautiful flowers, the stunning views and the trees. The only thing my guardian angel had thrown in for good measure was the wishing well – but who knows, there might have been one in the past. On seeing my meditation unfold before my very eyes, I tingled all over and thanked the angels for my premonition.

Now that we know we can reach the place of divine love within ourselves whenever we want to, there may also be times when we need healing for our heart and to feel more joy in life. This is a job for archangels.

❖ As you step out of your room, your guardian angel greets you. You may not always see or feel them clearly, but know that they are there to accompany you on your inner journey. First of all, your angel wants to give you some healing. As they raise their arms up to Heaven, a beautiful ray of light descends, surrounding both of you in divine healing and helping you to feel a stronger connection with your angel. It's as though you are as one within the light.

As the light fades, you find yourself in a stunning garden with your guardian angel still right by your side. You look around and see that everything appears to be in high definition, the flowers and trees practically sparkle and there is a beautiful aura around everything. Tiny dragonflies in the brightest colours you have ever seen dart from flower to flower. Deep purple butterflies rest on scented jasmine and birds of all different shapes, sizes and colours fly gently around the garden. It is a serene and peaceful scene.

Your angel guides you to a wooden bench under the shade of an old tree. Scented blossom is caught in the breeze and drifts down around you. This blossom is in the deepest yellow and lays a joyous carpet of yellow by your feet. You inhale its heady scent as you sit together for a while in silence, taking in the sights and sounds of the garden that stretches as far as the eyes can see.

After a short time, you see two figures in the distance. One is dressed in orange and white, the other in yellow. There is a golden light around them that moves with them. The figures come nearer now and you realise that they are large, magnificent archangels. Your guardian angel bows their head in respectful greeting and takes your hand as the archangels introduce themselves.

The one in orange and white steps forward, saying, "Welcome to the garden of the Divine. I am Archangel Haniel, the angel of the moon. Whenever you call on me, I will help to heal your emotional wounds by surrounding you in the grace of the Divine. I will help you to understand the truth from within and to live an abundant life. Call on me when the moon is full and I will bring you inner healing."

Now the angel in yellow says, "Welcome, I am Archangel Jophiel, the angel of beauty, wisdom and joy. I will bring enlightenment, laughter and joy into your life. I will raise your self-esteem as well as strengthening your communication skills. Know that you can call on me at any time of the day or night and I will be by your side. Notice the signs I leave for you once you call.

"In this moment, we want to show you around our garden. Everything about it is filled with the deepest joy and we want to share this with you. Come and look. Don't discount anything you see or feel, just allow yourself simply to be here." Archangel Jophiel tells you that you are beautiful as you are and starts to sing a lovely song. The vibration of the sound is so pleasing to your mind that you tingle all over, listening to the words and the melody.

Soon you notice that more angels have joined you, some small, some tall, some slim, some bigger. You realise that night has fallen while you have been here and the sky is a gallery of twinkling stars as a full moon lights up the garden with its magical energy that pulsates around you. You drink in its brilliance as you and the angels sing and dance. Let your inhibitions go, feel the loving grace of the angels, and have fun.

(Enjoy this feeling for five or six minutes.)

It is time to say your goodbyes. Your guardian angel wraps you in the healing white light again, and as the light slowly fades away you are back in your room. Sit down on your chair feeling it beneath you, wriggle your fingers and toes and, when you are ready, open your eyes. Take a drink of water.

Words that we share with loving intent really do help those in need, hearing with their souls. Praying to the angels is a beautiful and energising way of invoking their love and guidance as well as strengthening the bond between us. There are many prayers that will help us receive their celestial guidance so that we know which steps to take.

Remember though, human beings have been given the gift of free will by the Divine and we cannot expect the angels to do all the work! Only we ourselves can decide which choices to make in life and that's why a prayer to the angels helps because we are demonstrating our love and belief in their guidance and there is nothing more powerful than that. Bear in mind, too, that whatever we ask for will only be presented to us at the right time and if it's for our highest good.

Among the following prayers are some famous ones that you will recognise, and the rest are prayers I have written to help people on many levels, from releasing all that no longer serves them to moving forward with their divine life purpose.

- ❖ Angel of God, my guardian dear,
  to whom God's love commits me here,
  ever this day be at my side
  to light and guard, to rule and guide.
  Amen.

- ❖ Dear angels please help me rise above anything that no longer serves me and guide me to a place of peace. Please carry my worry and stress away on your mighty wings and

MEDITATION AND PRAYER

surround me with protection and strength. Let the darkness fade away so I may see the light as you allow me to feel your unconditional love within my heart so I may move forward at long last.
Thank you.

❖ Dear angels, please give me the courage to move away from the destructive actions of others in a natural way by never allowing anyone to cast a shadow over my dreams. Please send the right people into my life, those who have my best interests at heart and who will treat me as I deserve to be treated, with love, trust and affection.
Thank you.

❖ Dear angels, whenever I feel low alone or afraid, please comfort me through positive thoughts and actions. Send me a sign that you have heard my prayers and guide me towards new doors of love, opportunity and happiness.
Thank you.

❖ Dear angels, please protect me as I sleep and bless my dreams with messages I need to know at this time. Allow me to remember them as I awake so I may act upon them in the right way.
Thank you.

❖ Dear guardian angel, thank you for trusting in me throughout my life and guiding me along my life's path. I know that whenever I have taken a wrong turn it was a lesson for me to deal with in the right way, and it often resulted in something or someone special that was presented to me when I was eventually steered in the right direction. I feel blessed that we are connected through unconditional love and I believe in your presence always.
Thank you, dear guardian angel.

❖ Dear Archangel Gabriel, please help me with this situation [describe it]. Please guide those involved to make the right decision for the highest good of all as you shine your lantern of light to guide me. I thank you for ensuring a successful and happy outcome for all involved.
Thank you.

12
Afterlife

"Grief is the price we pay for love."
(Queen Elizabeth II)

Some of you may wonder why I have included accounts of our loved ones in the afterlife here. After all, they are not angels, although they are often described as being angelic because they always look out for us just as our guardian angels do. And it is the angels who help our loved ones to send us signs as proof that they live on in a different, peaceful and loving vibration within the universe. Some people describe this as 'going home'.

Equally, it is the angels who help those of us who are grieving as they are the ones who guide those who have gone before us towards the light when it's their time to transition from the Earth to the spirit world. So here you will read true stories of those who have received beautiful and comforting signs that have brought belief, beyond doubt, that when our loved ones pass on it is far from the end. And you will discover which angels to call on for help through the grieving process.

Moreover, one salient reason for including this chapter is because I was guided to do so by my own husband, who is now in the spirit world. John comes through in dreams and meditations regularly, still offering his sage advice as a spirit helper, and I wasn't going to ignore him!

These true life stories show that there are many different ways in which the angels help those in the afterlife to communicate with us. How can this happen? After all, they are in an entirely different vibration. Yet the answer is simple: the love they always had for us continues, as love transcends all boundaries and we are always connected by that love.

There is a beautiful Eskimo proverb that can help us feel at peace, knowing that we are never alone and that our loved ones are also at peace and free of any pain or discomfort.

> *"Perhaps those are not stars in the sky,*
> *but rather openings where our loved ones*
> *shine down to let us know they are happy."*

Grief can be all-encompassing and seemingly without end, even though people often say that "time will heal". It can be the hardest thing we have ever had to endure in our life, a relentless feeling of helplessness. Yet once we ask for divine assistance the angels will step in, whether it's to send the right people to comfort us through the waves of emotions that seem to come from nowhere, or to help loved ones in the spirit world to send definitive messages and signs of proof that they are alive and well.

Overseeing this work is Archangel Azrael, earlier described as 'the angel of death' because he helps the souls of those passing from this life to move on safely to the afterlife. However, this beautiful and caring angel doesn't stop there, because he knows how bereft those left on the Earth will be. So he is often also justly called 'the angel of grief', helping us through the trauma.

When our loved ones transition from this life to the next, they are sometimes described as 'gaining their wings'. Although they are not angels, it can often seem that way to us, thinking of them as being at peace in Heaven. It's a delicate subject. I would explain the difference this way: when our loved ones step from this life to the afterlife, they don't become angels because they have led a human life, unlike an angel who is a pure being of light. This will not, however, prevent our loved ones becoming guiding lanterns of light in our lives themselves.

Diane (as before, names have been changed to protect privacy) tells of the hardest thing that any mother could ever bear, the loss of her son Mark who killed himself. As she grieved for her beloved son, Diane went through extreme emotions such as shock, an immense sense of loss and disbelief, panic, confusion, as well as facing the painful question of why he had taken his own life. In her mind, if only she had known how much he was suffering, she might have been able to help and to prevent him making such a drastic and devastating decision.

Diane shared her story with me tearfully. One night a few days after Mark had passed away, she was sitting with her head in her hands absolutely distraught and sobbing. She shouted out to her son and all of a sudden she felt a change of energy in the room. Looking up, she saw the brightest white, radiant light edged with shimmering gold. And there, in the middle of the angelic light was her son. He came to her and put his hand on her shoulder, feeling warm and comforting.

"Mum, please don't worry about me," he said. "I am okay. It's not so bad here you know."

She rubbed her eyes but he was still there, this wasn't a dream. The angels had brought her son forward to prove he was living on in spirit and was now at peace. She was smiling now and described what had happened as breathtaking. After a short while, he and the light faded and he was gone, but his visit brought her so much solace to know that he was living on in the spirit world and was finally at peace. She was overjoyed by the experience and said he looked as handsome as ever.

A dramatic story of a loved one helping is that of my own Dad, who came forward in a powerful way during my time on the TV show *Rescue Mediums*. During this spirit rescue, both my co-host Jackie and I saw him as a much needed spirit helper, without realising at the time who it was.

It didn't take us long to recognise how difficult and emotional this episode was going to be from our initial premonitions, which we shared with each other before being taken to the haunted home. Looking back, there were many clues. One of them was that Jackie heard the name Joyce in her mind, my mother's name. But my Dad clearly wanted to maintain his anonymity throughout so as not to take the focus away from our work. However, during the investigation I kept hearing my name called and the voice seemed vaguely familiar. Jackie also kept smelling pipe tobacco and I could see wafts of smoke drifting into the air.

On the day of the spirit rescue, the cameras followed us from room to room capturing our every move as we encountered a very angry male spirit. We went into one of the bedrooms and sat on the bed. Suddenly I felt my feet rooted to the spot. I couldn't move as the agitated male spirit came forward and, with no warning, I felt myself being slapped hard around the face. My head shot backwards, then I felt immense pain in my hand and we both gasped in horror seeing my hand change shape, swelling up before our very eyes. I felt sick and my head was sore.

At this point, Jackie saw a small boy come forward and with each vision we finally understood that the adult male spirit and the small boy spirit were one and the same. As the light came in, he turned away from it reliving the horrendous physical abuse he had experienced as a child and that had haunted him all through his life, now continuing even after death. What he was experiencing was like a stuck record, a memory that kept him between worlds due to the cruel beatings he had experienced.

As rescue mediums, Jackie and I knew we had to move quickly because the energy was getting stronger. We decided to go to the basement of the property since it was the only room we hadn't yet walked around. As we descended the stairs it felt like walking into the bowels of the Earth. We sat down on a settee and Jackie said she could see a different male spirit standing in the corner of the room, smoking a pipe. But he was here as a gentle helper spirit and for that we were relieved.

When the furious spirit overshadowed me it was like being hit by a ton of bricks. One minute he was irate, the next desperate. Each emotion came fast and furious and I was already exhausted, yet I stayed with him as he changed back into a frightened little boy. I saw him cowering as he was hit relentlessly by an adult male that I didn't feel was family.

Watching this episode back is difficult for me even now because I saw myself as the spirit, crying and shouting out, "Don't let them do this to me. No, no, help me, I want my Mom! Please help me."

Jackie was brilliant, she calmed him down by talking to him gently as you would with any small child. He said he wanted his toy train and I felt someone hand me the toy – I could actually feel it in my hand – and it comforted the spirit. Jackie told him what he was experiencing was a bad memory that was playing over and over. She told him that he was safe now and no-one was going to hurt him. Then the gentle helper spirit came forward, guiding a lady towards the male spirit, his beloved mother that he had called out for before. She took his arm and together they went into the light. We both thanked our spirit helper as he followed, turned and waved to us.

It was only afterwards that Jackie and I realised it was my Dad who had helped with this very difficult spirit rescue. There had been my Mum's name, my own name being called gently, the pipe tobacco (Dad always smoked a pipe) and the toy train. My Dad loved trains and was an avid train spotter. However, the ultimate confirmation came as we relayed what had happened in the rescue to the homeowners at the end of the episode.

"Did your father smoke a pipe?" asked Lucille, the homeowner. Both she and her husband Norman had smelled pipe tobacco for the past few days so it seems my Dad had been there assessing the problem and working out how he could help before we had even got there! I was now sobbing on Jackie's shoulder with relief and thanks all rolled into one.

So who was the cruel person abusing the poor boy? We felt it was his tutor, as all the children of the family were taught at home. We didn't know if any of the other children were beaten or if it was just Henry, the name I was given in my premonition. But what we both felt during the investigation was the distress of a small defenceless boy being abused by a large adult male, feeling that he couldn't tell his parents because they wouldn't believe him.

Gloria is an intuitive medium and an important member of my small Rescue Mediums team, *The Tree of Life*, as she has helped send many earthbound spirits to the light here in Spain.

"When my husband passed away from cancer," she told me, "my Mum Dolly was a godsend. We are a close-knit family and she gave her support and made me feel less alone than I would have felt had she not been there. The rear of the house had been converted into a 'granny flat' so she would have her own personal space, yet I knew she felt lonely too since my Dad passed to spirit. As an only child I was very close to her and could tell her anything. We were always there for each other.

"At the age of ninety-two I could see how much she was struggling with her health and she had many hospital appointments. She got worse and I knew in my heart she wouldn't get better. I was caring for her at home but at times I had to ring for an ambulance as she was confused and in so much pain. Sometimes they kept her in overnight but on one occasion they brought her home at 3 a.m. in the morning!

"Every time I thought she was ready to go to spirit she kept holding on, until I realised that she was worried about me being on my own. So I gently told her that it was okay to go and, although I would miss her, I would be all right. She then said she'd been seeing a few of her ancestors around her bed for some time and this confirmed to me that it wouldn't be long before she transitioned.

"When she started to deteriorate, I sent a silent prayer up to my Dad in spirit asking him to help and I called the rest of the family here on Earth to come to the hospital as she wanted to see everyone. I knew without any doubt she was ready to go now. As I watched her saying her final farewells to the family, the room lit up and I knew the angels were with her. Even though I was so emotional, I felt angelic energy around me and was guided by the angels to open a beautiful coloured circular doorway, like a magical spiritual portal.

"I saw movement from the corner of the room and gasped because there was my Dad within the coloured light. He had heard my prayer and had come for her. Dad held out his arms to Mum and approached the bed to stroke her head. Then he took her hand and when the light in the room subsided I saw them standing at the end of the bed holding hands. They looked much younger as they turned to say goodbye. There were other spirit people following them too, the ancestors she had seen around her bed at home. I thanked Dad and watched them walk through the doorway between our worlds."

Kay told me a unique and uplifting story about what happened some time after her husband Steve had passed away. She was now in a new relationship and they were giving their first dinner party for friends. Moreover, Steve had always been the chef so she was quite nervous about that too.

While her guests were chatting, she popped outside to get some herbs from the garden and saw a little robin on the ground nearby. Afraid that the dogs might get it, she bent down and it hopped straight onto her finger! The little bird stayed there for a while as Kay talked to it, knowing it was a beautiful sign sent from her husband, telling Steve how much she loved him and about everything that had been happening in her life.

All the while, the robin had been sitting on her finger patiently until at last it shook itself and flew away. Kay said she was crying with both happiness and sadness at the same time, but knew in her heart that Steve was giving her his blessing that she had a new man in her life, sending the robin as confirmation.

Those who have gone before us sometimes make their presence felt very clearly. When Rita's father was dying in hospital, she took turns with her brothers and sister to sit with him so he wouldn't be alone. While at home, she lit a candle for her Dad and said a prayer, then saw a clear vision of his loving departed brother, Bill, standing in front of a dark triangle and also holding a candle. He spoke and said that this was so that her father would know the family were here and helping him to find his way.

Later that evening, she was sitting with her Dad in the hospital when her younger brother came to relieve her, and she told him about the vision she'd had earlier that day. At that exact moment, she felt something like an electric shock running through her body from her head right down to her legs. Her brother looked at her in surprise.

"You felt that as well, right?" he said. "The electricity through the body? I feel it too."

As the feeling subsided they stared at each other, knowing that Uncle Bill was telling them something. Their father passed away during the night.

Other spirits find unique – and sometimes not very 'spiritual' – ways of letting us know they are with us… Jennifer told me about her beloved brother, now in spirit.

"My brother had learning difficulties. He passed away when he was forty-five but only had a mental age of a five year-old. I know he's near when my Minion fart gun goes off randomly by itself, because he thought farts were hilarious. To see life through his eyes was always a privilege and I miss him so much."

We have extraordinary minds that can reach other dimensions and our dreams can even take us to the spirit worlds. Patti says that she was always close to her maternal grandmother, called Nanny, and they had lived together for a few months before Nanny moved to a nursing home. She passed away while Patti was training for the military; her mother told her that she had to finish her training but she felt guilty that she hadn't gone to the funeral.

For several years afterwards, Patti would have a recurring dream in which she saw Nanny and could talk to her. She didn't remember the conversations next morning yet always felt much happier. But then one night she had an especially powerful and vivid dream of being in a large, open area with many other people where there were big columns of flowers and all the people seemed to know one another. It seemed like a massive reception although Patti didn't recognise any of them. Then a young girl made her way to her through the crowd.

"You know that Nanny is with you always," she said, smiling. Patti then woke up, knowing that this was definite reassurance from Nanny from beyond the grave.

Delores also had a vivid dream in which she suddenly found herself at a door. She recognised it though, having arrived at this door twice before in dreams when she had been too frightened to open it and go in. This particular night, however, she found the courage to go through the door – to find her Dad looking at her. Even though it was a dream, she knew that she was meeting his spirit.

He tried to tell her something but she couldn't hear him clearly, it sounded as though his voice was coming from a distance and she told him this. So, instead, he then showed her a symbol she had never seen before. Intuitively, she felt it was connected with Reiki and asked him if this was correct. He nodded and told her telepathically that he was proud of her.

Delores realised that her father must have been with her earlier that very day as she was learning Reiki and had been practising with friends at college. She hadn't learned that particular symbol yet though, so the dream was confirmation for her that he was happy she had started out on her Reiki journey.

Our dreams can also predict the future although, interestingly, it's not always about our own lives. Sue says that when was working as a computer operator, her supervisor Pauline announced that she was going on holiday with a friend for a couple of weeks. Two nights later, Sue had a very realistic dream about Pauline's mother, whom she had never met. She was in a restaurant with her husband and casually said to him, "I am going now."

He seemed to assume that she meant she was going to the rest room, so he carried on looking at the menu as his wife slid under the table and died in the restaurant. Sue was shocked by how vivid the dream was and told the other girls she worked with about it, asking them not to mention it to Pauline when she came back from her holiday.

A few days later, the manager came to speak to them and said that Pauline wouldn't be back to work for a while as her mother had died while she was on holiday.

Rachael, too, had a dream that turned out to be very important concerning someone else. Amber had been her closest friend when they were growing up. They went through kindergarten together and even shared the same birthday, going side by side all the way through high school before later separating, as often happens, when different cliques formed and former friends divided. Rachael and Amber drifted apart and lost touch.

Many years later, Rachael heard that her old friend had got married and had a son, so she managed to track her down and called her to say congratulations and to say that she herself was pregnant with her first child. Then they lost touch again for a couple of years until Rachael heard that Amber's mother had died from brain cancer. She went to the funeral but couldn't stay long. And that was the last time she saw Amber, who herself died not long afterwards, also from brain cancer.

Despite living separate lives, that past deep friendship persisted and, a few years later, Rachael started having repetitive dreams about going on coffee dates with Amber. As they chatted, Amber kept mentioning her son, Ben, and saying she needed to get his attention, eventually pleading with Rachael to find him. In the last dream, she even called out to him saying, "Stop what you are doing! I can see it. Please stop hurting yourself."

Rachael was confused by this information. She didn't know Amber's son and had never spoken to him, yet the message was very clear and her friend's voice continued to haunt her until she knew she had to do her best to find him. She finally tracked him down on social media and relayed the dream she'd had, saying that it was his decision whether he wanted to believe it or not. She felt it was her job, out of loyalty to her friend, to pass on the message from his mother even though she had no idea what it meant except that she was clearly concerned about him. She could see what he was doing and it was extremely important to her that he knew this and that she still loved him very much.

A few days later, Rachael received a reply from Ben.

"Hello Rachael, I just want to say 'wow'! I want to thank you for passing Mom's message on to me. I was sold on the timing as I have been having a really rough time lately. Since I got your message it has made me happy and changed the way I was acting out. I can't thank you enough as Mom's message has had a huge impact on me because of the way my life was heading. It has helped me change my mindset and has been the biggest help I have had in the last two years. Thanks to you and my Mom."

So we see that our loved ones will often step in to support us when we are going through extreme difficulties. During the pandemic, Susan was a nurse doing an incredibly demanding job that was taking its toll on her and her colleagues. After several shifts in a Covid palliative care ward, she began to feel that she couldn't carry on.

"On the shuttle bus to the hospital one day," she said, "I had a panic attack and wanted immediately to get off when suddenly my Dad's voice came into my head, exactly as if he were actually there. He said, 'Have a word with yourself.' It was something he had said often, even though it sounds harsh, because he'd said this to himself when he was injured on a WWII battlefield at nineteen years-old. The message made me laugh out loud and the girl opposite me on the bus asked if I was okay. I said, yes, I was just 'having a moment'. I was able to carry on with my work, thanking my Dad for helping me through it all."

Similarly, Shannon told of a time when her father, who

had passed away a year before, saved her from a very dangerous situation. She was part of a ghost hunt investigation in Canada that was taking place in what had previously been the basement of an old jail. The main investigator had placed a 'ghost box' on the table, hoping that a spirit would communicate through it.

"I was standing at the back of the room on my own," Shannon said. "There was no-one around me and we were not receiving any spirit information from the ghost box. All of a sudden I heard a voice behind me shout, 'Grab the box.' I turned to see who had said this but there was no-one there. So I grabbed the ghost box and within seconds of holding onto it my Dad's voice came from the box saying, 'I am with you. But you need to get out, now!'

"I ran out, feeling as though I was going to be sick. But after a few minutes of catching my breath and grounding myself, I foolishly went back into the building. Immediately, I realised the investigator was provoking an evil spirit, trying to get his detection devices to respond. Somehow I knew something bad was going to happen.

"Sure enough, at that point the evil spirit started trying to push me back into that room. My back froze and I felt he was draining me of energy but I was determined not to go there. I knew my Dad was standing in front of me to protect me, too. I told the investigator he had to stop because someone would get hurt. Dad was there to make sure I was safe and that's why he had given me the warning at the start of the investigation."

I still find it hard to believe that my own beloved husband, John, has gone. He was my soulmate and the home is so empty without him. We knew he wouldn't make it because he was in so much pain, had lost a lot of weight and was completely incapacitated, not being able to walk or do anything for himself. None of the specialists he saw could help us either, we were just told it wasn't their area of expertise and they passed us on to someone else.

"I know this is the end for me," he said one evening, "I can feel it. But I am not scared of dying because of what you do. I know the angels will guide me." Tearfully, I told him I couldn't live without him and his reply was, "You will be okay. I will always be around you, I will find a way."

During the last five weeks of his life John was in hospital and every day I saw him deteriorating before my very eyes. I knew he couldn't carry on like that as he couldn't speak or swallow so I asked the angels to step in for the highest good of all. On the Monday, I saw a beautiful white light around his head that seemed to also light up his face and, two days later, on the Wednesday morning my beautiful man had passed away.

My family and friends took it in turns to come and stay with me. First was my friend Barbara who flew over on the day that John died. When she arrived she told me about a dream she'd had two nights earlier, on the Monday, the day I had seen the light around John's head. She said she hadn't understood the dream at the time.

"It was so vivid," she said, "I've never had a dream like that before. I saw John in a hospital gown running and running along the corridors of a hospital in bare feet. But he looked so happy and free, with a big smile on his face and the wires of a drip floating behind him."

I knew straight away that he had started to transition that day and the angels were guiding him, helping him to escape the earthly constraints that had tied him down for so long. He was on his way.

Three days later, Barbara was outside on the balcony and she shouted to me, "Ali, come and see this dragonfly." I ran out and couldn't see anything at first but just then it flew back around us and straight up into the sky, hovering as though looking down on us. I have never seen a dragonfly like it before, as big as a bird and a golden colour. It stayed there for ages in the sky until it swooped down over our heads and was gone.

This was a message from John. He loved dragonflies and this one was magical, not least because this was a cold day in January. John said he would find a way and he did. But he wasn't finished yet…

A week later, my friend Pam came to stay. Halfway through the week I decided to scatter John's ashes and felt guided to invoke the natural elements of life, fire, air, earth and water. Some ashes were scattered in the sea, some in our garden, some were carried away by the breeze and I placed some in candles as I lit them, all the while speaking to John. As I invoked the element of air, a beautiful Red Admiral butterfly landed right in front of me and stayed there as I called Pam to come and see it. The butterfly waited, flew around my head and then Pam's before finally flying away.

Later in the day when I came into the house from the garden, I heard the song *Lady in Red* playing on the smart speaker. I asked Pam why she had asked for the song but she had no idea what I was talking about – she was busy on her phone. That song was very special to John and me. When we first met at a Christmas party, I was wearing a red dress so that's what John called me.

Neither Pam nor I had asked for the song, but we knew who had!

My editor wants to have the last word…

I have personally been a bit sceptical about some of Alison's beliefs, especially regarding feathers as angelic signs. Well, when I was working from home, editing this book and coming towards the end, I paused for a moment and spoke aloud to John, whom I had met once years before.

"Have I done a good job for Alison?" I asked.

I then went into the kitchen to get a drink. Stuck in the very middle of the window was a fluffy white feather.

Addendum

"Babies and children are angels who sprinkle magic dust on your heart."
(Author unknown)

Just like angels, babies and children are pure. Being so young, they don't question what they believe in, even if they can't see it. Their minds are open and they say exactly what they feel. So whether it's the tooth fairy, dragons and wizards, Santa Claus or angels, they trust what they feel and that makes them happy rather than analysing everything, which happens as we grow up and are conditioned by life.

I posted on social media for those with young children in the family to ask them the question, "What is an angel?", and I was inundated with messages that made me laugh and cry, warming my heart. Here are some of them (names have been changed to protect their privacy).

Molly (aged four)

"Molly, what is an angel?"
"An angel is a cat." (The family has a cat called Angel.)
"Do they have wings"
"Yes, and they wear white."
"Are angels special?"
"Yes they are special, and they don't talk but I don't know why. But they do talk inside."
"What do you mean by inside?"
"They talk inside my head. We have angels in our house too. They protect us so the monsters don't get us."

Tilly (aged three)

"An angel is a person who smells of flowers."

Ryan (aged six)

"An angel said when you are good God makes you an angel."

William (aged nine)

"My Dad is an angel now who watches over me."
William's Dad died when he was two years-old and yet even then he would say that his Dad woke him up during the night to read him a story.

Evie (aged five)

"All the dogs who have died are angels now in Heaven."

Thomas (aged six)

"An angel is like a wishbone in a chicken. When you wish for something the angel helps it come true."

Charlotte (aged six)

"Angels are magical and nice. They glow and help people. Fairies and angels are in Heaven. They are on the Earth too, but there are more of them in Heaven."

Olivia (aged twelve)

"An angel is a divine creature that is sent from Heaven to deliver goodness to the Earth."

ADDENDUM

Charlie (aged nine)

"A person that flies and gives you good luck and guides us to the gates of Heaven."

Taylor (aged seven)

"It's like a type of guide that protects people with good and kind words."

Blakely (aged ten)

"God's friend and always surrounding you."

Kennedy (aged twelve)

"They are partners with God to help people who are struggling and there are different types of angels such as guardian angels. I hope I have a special angel but I don't know her name. One time when I was younger I had a dream where I was talking to a lot of people I knew and I met a guardian angel but I wasn't sure if it was my angel or someone else's."

Judson (aged five)

"I dunno! I have seen a boy angel in my bed. His name was Max. He came to see me when I lost my tooth."

Natalie (aged eleven)

"An angel is a fairy wearing a dress with a halo."

Charlie (aged four)

"An angel is very kind and helps people. They are kind like Jesus and sometimes they are fairy angels."

Children take such comfort in believing about the angels. They say what they feel and with no filters! But I'm sure we wouldn't have it any other way.

If you have enjoyed this book...

Local Legend is committed to publishing the very best spiritual writing, both fiction and non-fiction. You might also enjoy:

THE QUIRKY MEDIUM
Alison Wynne-Ryder (ISBN 978-1-907203-47-3)

Alison has been the co-host of the TV show *Rescue Mediums*, in which she put herself in real danger to free homes of lost and often malicious spirits. Yet she is a most reluctant medium, afraid of ghosts! This is her amazing and often very funny autobiography, taking us back stage of the television production as well as describing how she came to discover the psychic gifts that have brought her an international following.

Winner of the Silver Medal in the national *Wishing Shelf Book Awards*.
"Almost impossible to put down."

LOVE, DEATH AND BEYOND
Helen Ellwood (ISBN 978-1-910027-51-6)

Helen had always been almost afraid of living, believing that mere dark oblivion awaited her in the end. Trained in medical sciences and having rejected religious beliefs, she often felt terrified. But Beryl the hamster changed everything when her soul rose from her body at death, and Helen was shocked into opening herself to the spiritual and the numinous. The paranormal experiences came one after another now and it was soon clear that the human mind was far more powerful, and consciousness far more enduring, than she had imagined. Every reader will identify with the author's doubts and fears, and be inspired by this beautifully written memoir.

Winner of the national *Spiritual Writing Competition.* and Bronze Medal in the *Wishing Shelf Book Awards*
"…compelling… intriguing…" with score 94%

PAST LIFE HEALING
Judy Sharp (ISBN 978-1-910027-52-3)

Do we live many lives – and could trauma of the past still be affecting our health and wellbeing here and now? The author was completely healed of her own severe claustrophobia in one session and now has decades of professional experience helping others with issues from fear of flying to stubborn weight gain. This truly eye-opening book gives many evidential case studies, alongside a wealth of information about the concept of past lives across history and different cultures, as well as details of the extensive research carried out in this field.

Winner of the national *Spiritual Writing Competition.*
"A fascinating insight… highly recommended!"
Wishing Shelf Book Awards

GHOSTS OF THE NHS
Glynis Amy Allen (ISBN 978-1-910027-34-9)

It is rare to find an account of interaction with the spirit world that is so wonderfully down-to-earth! The author simply gives us one extraordinary true story after another, as entertaining as they are evidential. Glynis, an hereditary medium, worked for thirty years as a senior hospital nurse in the National Health Service, mostly in A&E wards. Almost on a daily basis, she would see patients' souls leave their bodies escorted by spirit relatives or find herself working alongside spirit doctors – not to mention the Grey Lady, a frequent ethereal visitor! A unique contribution to our understanding of life, this book was an immediate bestseller.
Winner of the SILVER MEDAL in the national
Wishing Shelf Awards.
"What a fascinating read. The author has a way of putting across a story that is compelling and honest… highly recommended!"

THE ANGELS BESIDE US
Glynis Amy Allen (ISBN 978-1-910027-39-4)

A sequel to *Ghosts of the NHS*, Glynis gives us more eye-opening accounts of her spiritual experiences in her inimitably humble and honest style. Here we read of her many encounters with beautiful and compassionate angelic beings who come to guide us when in danger or to give comfort to the sick. Her life has been dedicated to working in the NHS and with Spirit, and she shares her vast knowledge of the ethereal worlds with us, teaching us how we may reach out to and work with our own guardian angels. This book is warmly endorsed by the renowned 'angel author' Chrissie Astell.
Winner of the national *Spiritual Writing Competition.*

THE SOUL CAVE
Sandra Francis (ISBN 978-1-910027-57-8)

Every one of us, Sandra believes, has far greater ability and energy than we realise and in everyday life we only use a small part of our extraordinary minds. We each have the power to create the happy, fulfilled and peaceful lives our souls crave and deserve. Yes, life has many challenges, but we can rise above them and turn them to our advantage, healing the pain of past events and forming new, better relationships. And it's never too late…

Sandra is proof of this. Despite illness and trauma, in middle age she set out on a spiritual path of loving acceptance, forgiveness and gratitude that completely changed her life. In this beautifully written book, she shows us all the way.

SPIRIT SHOWS THE WAY
Pam Brittan (ISBN 978-1-910027-28-8)

A clairvoyant medium for over thirty years and highly respected throughout the UK, Pam describes herself as "an ordinary woman with an extraordinary gift." Despite many personal difficulties, she has shared this gift tirelessly and brought comfort and understanding of the Spirit to a great many people. Here, she inspires us to realise our own innate gifts and to trust that Spirit will always guide us on the right path.

TWO SISTERS
Graham Adrian (ISBN 978-1-910027-32-5)

Graham's debut novel, based on a Suffolk legend, is a brilliant, historically accurate description of Georgian times including genuine dialect. But far more than this, it is a truly exciting – and uniquely spiritual – adventure story. Nance is an honest and hard-working farmer's daughter, but falling in love only begins a sequence of devastating events that seem to lead inevitably to the gallows! Yet she is watched over by her sister's loving spirit in the afterlife, doing all she can to avert the consequences of Nance's reckless decisions. Every character in this gripping story, illustrated with period images, will be profoundly changed by its final chapter.

"A well-crafted historical plot with strong characterisation and dialogue which reflects the place and time."
The *Wishing Shelf Book Awards*

THE HOUSE OF BEING
Peter Walker (ISBN 978-1-910027-26-4)

Acutely observed verse by a master of his craft, showing us the mind, the body and the soul of what it is to be human in this glorious natural world. A linguist and a priest, the author takes us deep beneath the surface of life and writes with sensitivity, compassion and, often, with searing wit and self-deprecation. This is a collection the reader will return to again and again.

A winner of the national *Spiritual Writing Competition*.

SPIRIT REVELATIONS
Nigel Peace (ISBN 978-1-907203-14-5)

With descriptions of more than a hundred proven prophetic dreams and many more everyday synchronicities, the author shows us that, without doubt, we can know the future and that everyone can receive genuine spiritual guidance for our lives' challenges. World-renowned biologist Dr Rupert Sheldrake has endorsed this book as "…vivid and fascinating… pioneering research…"

A national runner-up in *The People's Book Prize* awards.

ODD DAYS OF HEAVEN
Sandra Bray (ISBN 978-1-910027-17-2)

If you feel that you've lost the joy in your life and are not sure where you're going, this book is written for you. Sandra knows those feelings all too well. Rocked by mid-life events, she refused to be a victim of circumstances and instead resolved to treat them as opportunities for change and growth. She looked for a spiritual 'guide book' to offer her new thoughts and activities for each day, but couldn't find one – so she wrote it! In this book, and her sequel *Even More Days of Heaven*, we find almost four hundred brilliantly researched suggestions, sure to life our spirits.

Runner-up in the national *Spiritual Writing Competition*.

Local Legend titles are available worldwide as paperbacks and eBooks.
Further details and extracts of these and many
more beautiful books for the Mind, Body and Spirit
may be seen at

https://local-legend.co.uk

www.ingramcontent.com/pod-product-compliance
Lightning Source LLC
Chambersburg PA
CBHW060154050426
42446CB00013B/2817